Cambridge English Readers

Level 6

Series editor: Philip Prowse

T0275212

The Best of Times?

Alan Maley

'It was the best of times, it was the worst of times.'
A Tale of Two Cities by Charles Dickens

CAMBRIDGE
UNIVERSITY PRESS

University Printing House, Cambridge CB2 8BS, United Kingdom

Cambridge University Press is part of the University of Cambridge.

It furthers the University's mission by disseminating knowledge in the pursuit of education, learning and research at the highest international levels of excellence.

www.cambridge.org
Information on this title: www.cambridge.org/9780521735452

First published 2009
Reprinted 2016

Alan Maley has asserted his right to be identified as the Author of the Work in accordance with the Copyright, Designs and Patents Act 1988.

Printed in the United Kingdom by Hobbs the Printers Ltd

Typeset by Aptara Inc.
Map artwork by Malcolm Barnes

A catalogue record of this book is available from the British Library.

ISBN 978-0-521-73545-2 Paperback

My thanks go to many friends and colleagues in Malaysia for their advice and most particularly to Stephen Hall, Lee Ming Chen, Lee Su Kim, Jayakaran Mukundan, Zarina Mustafa and to Savanhkeo Kanlaya for the loan of her laptop! Any shortcomings are my own.

Contents

Characters

Chee Seng: a sixteen-year-old Malaysian boy
Sammy Yeo: Chee Seng's father
Linda Yeo (Wei Fong): Chee Seng's mother
Auntie Swee Eng: a kind elderly relative
Uncle Krish (Krishnan): a close friend of the Yeo family
Auntie Veena: Krish's wife
Puri (Purissima): the Yeo family's Filipina maid
Jessica: Chee Seng's girlfriend
Jane: Jessica's elder sister
Dev (Devinder), Faisal and Ka Choon: Chee Seng's three closest school friends
Ka Ting: a rich classmate of Chee Seng

Malaysia stretches from Thailand in the north to the islands of Singapore and Indonesia in the south. It also includes Sarawak and Sabah on the island of Borneo.

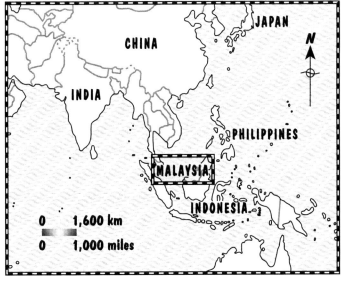

Chapter 1   *Visiting time*

I am not frightened. No, not me. I'm terrified! I hate the smell of hospitals – that mixture of disinfectant and human waste and stale bodies – and fear. And I don't know what I'll find when I see her. My mother, I mean. Luckily, Auntie Swee Eng is with me. There's something comforting about her. She makes me feel safe, even when these terrible things are happening. Of course, she's old – but somehow that doesn't matter. I know that she'll help me to face whatever it is that waits for me behind that white door.

The nurse in her smart white uniform calls us over and pushes open the door to the private room. Auntie Swee Eng gives me her warm hand and together, hand in hand, we go into the room. Suddenly I think how strange it is – I'm only sixteen but I tower over the tiny figure of Auntie Swee Eng, who must be at least fifty years older than me. But, tall as I am, I'm still terrified. Thank goodness she's with me. She may be old and small, but she seems so strong. She's tough all right!

After the bright lights of the corridor outside, we find ourselves in the darkness of the room. It takes a few moments before I can see anything. Then, gradually, my eyes get used to the darkness, and objects start to come into focus – the bed and the bedside table with a glass on it; the plastic curtains open by the bed; the dark shape lying under the sheets with tubes coming out of its nose and arms, connected to the frame with a bottle hanging from it; the machine next to the bed with red and green lights; the small table with medicine bottles and metal trays on it; a chair by the bed; the temperature chart hanging on the end of the bed; the sink in the corner; the dark shape of a wardrobe next to the door. The dim outline of a window is visible, but the dark green curtains are closed, so it looks like a TV screen which has been switched off.

Auntie Swee Eng and I stand for a moment just inside the door. The shape on the bed doesn't move but we can hear the faint sound of breathing, and as our eyes get used to the darkness, we can see the sheets rising and falling. We move silently towards the bed. Auntie Swee Eng makes me sit on the chair. Is this my mother? All I can see is the pale outline of a face and the white hospital nightdress. Her eyes are closed. I can see a tube fastened to her arm and a tube which goes into her nose. I take her hand. Her skin feels like dry paper. There's no movement. It's like holding a child's doll, loose and lifeless. But, just as I'm about to let go, I feel her hand squeeze mine – a small movement but it's a sign of life. Yet her eyes are still closed. Her face still does not move. I feel as if she's on another planet, drifting away from me. Is this really my mother? Is this really happening?

How did this all happen? Why is she here, fighting for her life? Is it my fault? What did I do wrong? What did we all do wrong to come to this? I start to feel panic. I feel a mixture of sadness, hopelessness and anger. She must be very ill because she's in the intensive care unit. I feel sick and dizzy from thinking about it. I just cannot think straight. I cannot breathe. I need air. I can't stay here in this enclosed atmosphere any more. I have to get out.

And everything has happened so fast. They only released me from the police station this morning. It was Auntie Swee Eng who came to collect me and take me here. Now I've seen Mum, I realise just how wrong I've been about so many things.

'Come on, Chee Seng, I think we'd better go now,' says Auntie Swee Eng softly. She seems to know and understand how I'm feeling. I take a last look at the dark shape of my mother on the hospital bed, then follow Auntie Swee Eng into the blinding light of the corridor.

The nurse takes us to a cool, quiet waiting room. She brings us some cold drinks. 'Don't worry,' says Auntie Swee Eng. 'The doctor will come to see us when he finishes with his other patients.'

Chapter 2   *The best of times*

As I sit there in that impersonal, white waiting room, I start to think about our life together. My family, I mean. What happened to us? When did things start to go wrong?

Until about a year ago everything was perfect – or at least, that's how it seemed to me. Dad was doing well in his job. They'd just promoted him to export manager at Intercorp, where he worked. At weekends we often went off somewhere together. We had a nice house in a green suburb of Kuala Lumpur called Subang Jaya. At weekends, Mum and Dad often had friends over for lunch or dinner or parties. My parents – Mr Sammy Yeo and Linda – were a popular couple. Whenever I think of our times together, they seem to be bathed in a golden light in my memory.

While I was growing up, Dad was really the centre of my world. He was a wonderful father and was always there for me.

Most days, after work, he would take me up to the park at the top of our street to play football or help me practise my basketball skills. He was always around to help me with my homework, especially maths. He was a wizard at maths, no wonder he'd been promoted. Most nights he would read to me in bed before I went to sleep. Once he read me the whole of *The Lord of the Rings* – it took him months to finish it! He taught me to swim too and arranged tennis lessons. Everything I remember about him glows with that warm, golden light. Even now, after everything that's happened.

So when did it all start? I think back to my last birthday. I was sixteen and Mum and Dad had organised a big party for me. Mum came from a large family and so did Dad, so the house was filled with uncles and aunts and cousins from all over the place. And that wasn't all, because both Mum and Dad had loads of friends too; who I called 'Uncle' and 'Auntie', even though they weren't really. Of course, Auntie Veena and Uncle Krish were there. They were Mum and Dad's closest friends.

Then there were my best friends from school – Dev, Faisal and Ka Choon. Dev, short for Devinder, was Indian-Malaysian. He lived just up the same street in Subang Jaya. Dev was a great sportsman, especially at hockey. Faisal lived just round the corner from us. He came from a Malay family. And Ka Choon was Chinese-Malaysian. He lived miles away in a very expensive neighbourhood. We were all very different, but that didn't stop us from being the best of friends.

Mum was a great cook and so were all her friends, so there were all sorts of special dishes that they'd brought to the party. Our Indian friends came round with *samosas*[1] and curries of all descriptions. Malay friends arrived with *satay*[2] and peanut sauce, and spicy beef *rendang*[3]. Chinese friends and relatives brought along Hainan chicken rice, spicy Szechuan tofu[4] and Peking duck served with paper-thin pancakes. Our Straits Chinese relatives, Auntie Swee Eng and Auntie Rosie, brought Peranakan dishes like *asam laksa*[5] – that was one of my real favourites, with its sour tamarind[6] taste and spicy fish soup. And to top it all, Mum brought in an enormous birthday cake with sixteen candles.

Yet, though everything was perfect, something didn't feel quite right. Once or twice I caught Mum looking strangely at Auntie Veena. Auntie Veena was Indian-Malaysian. She was really beautiful. When she was younger she'd been chosen as Beauty Queen of Selangor[7] State, and you could see why. On my birthday she was wearing a dark red silk sari[8] with a gold border, with white jasmine flowers in her hair. Mum was good-looking too, but not in the same way. Uncle Krishnan was quite the opposite. He had a bald head and a big fat stomach. Sometimes I wondered why Auntie Veena had married him. But he was a lot of fun and he was Dad's best friend from school and university. Mum and Auntie Veena got on well too, always laughing and joking as they did things together. Before Mum married Dad, she'd worked in the company owned by Veena's father. That's when they first became friends. The four of them spent a lot of time together, especially at weekends. And that's why Veena and Krishnan were there at my party.

Then I remembered something else too. After we'd had the wonderful food and cut the cake, I went off to my room with my friends to play the video games they'd brought me as presents. All the adults settled down to relax and chat on the terrace outside and in the lounge. Some of them fell asleep in their chairs. It was that sleepy time after a heavy meal.

After a while, I decided to go downstairs to get some cool drinks for my friends. As I came out of my room, I saw Dad and Auntie Veena on the stairs. They were looking at each other in a way I'd never seen before, and Dad had his hand on her bare arm. He quickly took it away when he saw me. They looked embarrassed, and Dad went upstairs mumbling something to me as he passed. Auntie Veena hurried downstairs again.

We went back to our games and I didn't think much about what I'd seen. And I forgot about it completely when Dad came in later carrying a big basket. I heard a scratching sound inside, and when he opened it, there was the little black and white dog I'd wanted for so long.

'What shall we call him?' Dad asked.

'Let's call him Raj,' I answered.

Everyone clapped as Raj barked his agreement. It was a perfect day. And from then on, Raj was my best and most faithful friend.

But now, as I sit here in the hospital, waiting for the doctor and thinking about Dad, that other strong image blacks out my brain. The bedroom, the cries, the bodies moving on my parents' bed. I am powerless to stop that image from coming back. It is burnt on my memory like the mark an iron leaves on a shirt. How did it all happen? Why did it all happen? Why couldn't we have gone on living in the best of times for ever? These black thoughts flood my mind again. I feel the tears in my eyes. Auntie Swee Eng can see how upset I am. She takes my hand and gives it a squeeze. I look up at the clock. When will the doctor come?

Chapter 3 *The worst of times*

The hands on the clock move so slowly as I sit on that uncomfortable chair in the waiting room. I keep trying to remember how things changed after my birthday party. There wasn't one particular thing I remember, but just a lot of small things. Teenagers pick up a lot – from the atmosphere and from what goes on around them. Sometimes it's just a vague feeling of unease, a feeling that something is not quite right, a feeling that things have changed in a way you can't describe, yet it's a feeling that's real. And that's how it was for me, I think, in those months after my birthday. It was like a virus – something sick in the air, invisible but definitely there. It's only now, when I think back on everything, that I can see the pattern. At the time, it was no more than a vague, nervous feeling deep down in my stomach, a feeling of threat, of insecurity, that gradually replaced my feelings of innocent happiness.

I noticed that Dad started coming home later and later from the office. Mum made excuses for him but I could see she wasn't happy about it. Neither was I! It meant that he was never there to play football or basketball up in the park. In fact, I hardly ever saw him. He left early and came back after I'd gone to bed. It felt wrong somehow. I was so used to being with him. It left a big gap in my life now that he was too busy to think about me.

'He's got a big new product coming out next month,' Mum said when I asked her. But then the next month came, and the next, and he still came back late.

One day I came back from school and Mum wasn't around to welcome me as she usually was. After a while, she came out of the bedroom. Her eyes were red and swollen, and I knew she'd been crying. 'What's up, Mum?' I asked.

'It's nothing,' she answered in a strange, tense voice. 'I just have a lot on my mind at the moment. It's OK, nothing for you to worry about.' She put on a brave smile. 'Now, let me make you some noodles[9] with seafood sauce. Or would you like something else?'

She called Purissima, our Filipina maid, from the servant's room, and together they went to the kitchen. I liked Puri (that was her nickname; Purissima is too long to say all the time). She was small and neat, and always seemed to have a bright smile, especially for me. She spoiled me a lot – always making me my favourite dishes. I especially remember her voice. Her accent always made her Filipina English sound a bit American.

'What you want for your dinner?' she would ask, rolling the 'r' sounds in 'your' and 'dinner'. 'Today I make you something special for your dessert – from my home town. Made from *taro*[10]. Is very sweet. I think you like.' And I always did like it. Whatever it was!

But these days even Puri seemed to have changed. She was quieter and didn't smile as much as before. Sometimes she even looked worried.

'Is anything wrong?' I asked her one day.

But she just smiled and said, 'Oh no. I get some headache, make me feel not so good. Is OK. I make you some special spaghetti, or you want a pizza? I can make for you. Special one.'

But later on that day, when I came down from my room, she was on the phone to her Indonesian friend Henny, who worked for a family in the next street. '… now the boy, he also see something wrong. I don' know how to do. What you think?'

There was a silence while her friend answered. Then she went on, 'Oh no. Cannot. Is bad for him. But Madam, she cry every day. And Master, sometimes he comes so late. Then I hear fight starting …'

Suddenly, she noticed I was there. 'Oh, I got to go now. I talk again later,' she whispered, and put the phone down quickly. 'OK, now I go make something nice for you, something special,' she said with an embarrassed smile, and rushed off to the kitchen.

* * *

As the weeks went by, I noticed how quiet the house had become. There were no more parties, and Uncle Krish and Auntie Veena never came over now. We never seemed to go anywhere together at weekends either, like we had before. Sometimes Dad was out all day on Saturday or Sunday. Other times he stayed in his study room with the door closed. I was uneasy and confused about all this, so one day I decided to ask Mum. It was a difficult decision because I'd always been closer to Dad. But now she was the only one I could ask.

'Mum, why can't we go out somewhere on Saturday, like we used to? I don't like to stay at home all the time.'

'You'd better ask your father,' she said angrily. I think that was the first time Mum had ever spoken to me like that. She made me feel as if I'd done something wrong by even asking that question.

'But why can't we?'

'I told you. Ask your father. It's got nothing to do with me.'

'Well, can't we ask Auntie Veena and Uncle Krish over? We never see them now. They haven't been over for ages. We never have any fun.'

The way she looked at me stopped me from asking anything else. Her eyes were flashing furiously and her whole body was shaking with anger.

' "Fun"? Did you say "fun"? Don't talk to me about "fun". You'd better ask your father about that too!' She almost spat the words out at me. 'And get that dog out of here. He's always under my feet!'

I felt so miserable that I went straight to my room. When I came down for dinner, my mother had already gone to my parents' bedroom.

* * *

A few nights later, I heard Dad's car in our drive. The car door banged shut and the front door opened. Then I heard Mum's voice. She wasn't shouting, probably because she didn't want to wake me up, but her whispering voice was really intense, like the hissing of a snake. I went to my bedroom door to hear better.

'How can you come back so late? Don't think I don't know where you've been – again!'

'Why don't you just shut up and go to bed?' My father answered back. It sounded hard and unpleasant. I'd never heard my parents speak to each other like that before. In fact, they always spoke to each other in a loving way. They always called each other '*abang*' or '*sayang*', which means 'beloved' or 'darling' in Malay. But as I listened, I realised that I hadn't heard any *sayang*s or *abang*s for a long time.

'I won't put up with this any more. You'd better make up your mind,' my mother hissed.

'Don't push me!' Dad's voice was full of anger. 'Who do you think you are? I look after both of you. You have this house, your car, money, everything. What more do you want? Think yourself lucky!'

I heard them coming upstairs so I quickly went back to bed. I could hear them still arguing in their bedroom. There was a loud bump and a slap. Then silence.

I didn't sleep until it was almost morning and time for me to get ready for school. Dad had already left. When Mum came down to see me off, I noticed that one eye was swollen and she had a red mark on her cheek. I didn't ask her any questions that time. There was no need.

* * *

The following Saturday, Mum had to go to Melaka to see her old Aunt Mei Ling, who was sick in hospital. Dad was supposed to be working, and it was Puri's weekend off. Mum had made arrangements for me to sleep over at my friend Ka Choon's place.

But it didn't work out like that. I had a silly argument with Ka Choon and decided not to stay at his place. Around ten in the evening I took a taxi home. Dad's car was in the drive but the house was in darkness, except for the light shining on the terrace. I found my keys and let myself in.

For some reason I didn't switch on the lights in the lounge downstairs. There was enough light from the terrace to see, and as I went up the stairs my eyes got used to the darkness. As I was going towards my bedroom, I suddenly became aware of voices – a man's and a woman's – coming from my parents' bedroom at the end of the corridor. For a moment, I thought maybe Mum had come back early from Melaka. But these were no ordinary voices. They sounded wild, out of control, a flood of cries and crazy laughter rising and falling in waves of excitement; and words – words I knew about but had never heard spoken like that before.

I walked silently to the bedroom door. It was half-open. I couldn't stop myself – I looked in quickly. In the dim light I could see the outline of two bodies moving on the bed. I can still see their shapes in my mind's eye, and hear their words and their passionate cries. They were too busy with each other to notice me, but I shall never be able to forget what I saw. I realised that the woman's voice was not my mother's – it belonged to Auntie Veena …

After that everything fell apart.

Chapter 4 *The aftershock*

I don't know how I got through that night. All I can remember is going back to my room and locking the door. My mind was frozen. I was in a state of deep shock. I couldn't think. Every time I closed my eyes I saw the shape of those two bodies on the bed. It was like a film which goes on playing the same scene over and over. I must have slept eventually because when I woke up, Dad's car had gone.

I spent all of Sunday morning alone in the house. I felt confused, shocked, and disgusted – all mixed up together. I thought I should eat something but when I opened the fridge, the smell of food sickened me. I couldn't face going to the park to be with my friends. What could I say to them?

Poor Raj. He kept running around, crying and following me everywhere. He couldn't understand what was wrong. I turned on the TV and sat in front of it, my eyes staring, not really watching. Raj climbed on the sofa and put his head on my knee. I was still there when Puri came back at 5 pm.

'You all alone?' she asked. I nodded. 'Your dad gone out or what?' I nodded again. 'Never mind. Your mum will be back soon. I make you something to eat, OK?'

'No thanks, Puri,' I muttered. I tried not to cry, but I suddenly realised that the tears were pouring down my face and my shoulders were shaking uncontrollably.

'What's wrong with you, Chee Seng? Something happen?' How could I answer that question? I was too ashamed to tell her what had happened. 'Come on, it's not so bad,' she said, and gave me a big hug. I felt better with her warm arms around me. She had three kids of her own back in the Philippines, so I guess she felt motherly to me too. She sent me to the bathroom to wash my face. Then she sat me at the kitchen table, while she prepared some sliced mango[11] with my favourite sticky rice. I started to feel a bit better.

* * *

Everything changed again when Mum came back at 8 pm. She rushed through the door like a tropical storm. 'Where's your father?' she demanded angrily. She didn't even greet me. I didn't answer. 'I asked you a question!' she screamed, 'Don't you dare look at me like that!'

'I don't know…' I mumbled softly. I felt sure she was expressing her anger with Dad, but it was hitting me instead!

'What do you mean, you don't know?' she went on. 'You've been here, haven't you?'

She didn't stay for an answer but rushed upstairs to their bedroom. I followed her quietly and stood outside the open door. She was standing by the window. The bed was still unmade, the sheets untidy. The drawers and the wardrobe doors were all open and clothing was thrown around on chairs and on the floor. I could see that Dad's suits weren't hanging in the wardrobe any more. And his laptop had gone from the table where it usually was. There was an open empty suitcase abandoned in one corner.

'So it's true, he's gone!' she said – to herself, not to me. 'My God, he's gone…' She started to cry. I wanted to go and hug her but something warned me not to enter the room. 'You coward!' she screamed. 'After all I've done for you. I can't believe it! Running off with that… dirty creature! And not even brave enough to tell me to my face, just leaving a message on my phone!'

She collapsed onto a chair, holding her head in her hands, crying uncontrollably. 'What am I going to do?'

I pulled together all my courage and went in to her. I tried to hold her but she pushed me away angrily. 'Get away from me! Don't you dare come in here. Get out of my sight. Now! Right now! Do you hear me?'

I'd never seen Mum like that before and I ran out of the room, shaking. I was suddenly afraid of this fierce stranger, a wild animal that threatened me in my own home, no longer recognisable as Mum. It was as if she was blaming me. I couldn't stand it. I ran to my room and locked the door.

A few minutes later I heard her speaking on the phone. Her voice sounded tired and weak. 'Swee Eng? Can I see you? I need to talk to you …' There was a pause. 'No, I mean now. I know it's late but it's important …' Another pause. 'I can't tell you on the phone, I'm sorry …'

Her voice started to shake and I guessed she was crying again. 'I'm really desperate, Swee Eng. Please come over.' Another pause. 'Thanks so much. I don't know what I'd do without you. I'll see you soon.' She put the phone down.

Not long after, I heard Auntie Swee Eng's car in the drive. I called her Auntie but she was not really my aunt, although she was somehow related to us by marriage. I could never work out exactly what the relationship was, but I think her sister had married one of Mum's cousins. Auntie Swee Eng was a Peranakan *nyonya*[12] like Mum, and very proud of it too. I don't know how old she was, but she always dressed very smartly in her *kebaya*[13] blouse and carefully wrapped *sarong*[14]. Her grey hair was always tied neatly at the back of her head.

She was small but full of intense energy, like a bright-eyed bird. I liked her a lot. She was one of those adults who always took me seriously, always listened to what I had to say, and always had a kind word of encouragement.

I didn't dare go downstairs after the way Mum had shouted at me. But I really wanted to know what Mum and Swee Eng were talking about. I opened my door carefully and walked quietly to the top of the stairs. I couldn't hear very clearly but I caught bits and pieces of their conversation.

'So when did all this start?' That was Auntie Swee Eng. I couldn't make out Mum's reply. 'Do you think he'll come back?' Auntie Swee Eng asked.

'I don't want him back!' That was Mum all right!

'But how are you going to manage?' Again I didn't catch Mum's reply. 'There's no reason to blame yourself, my dear. These things happen, you know. It's not your fault. But what about Chee Seng?' Again, I missed the answer. 'I'll do whatever I can to help you, Wei Fong.' It sounded strange to hear her use Mum's Chinese name. I only knew her as Mum, Dad usually called her *sayang*, and most other people just called her by her European nickname, Linda.

Their voices went on, rising and falling, but it became more and more difficult for me to follow what they were saying. I think I must have been exhausted from everything that had happened. Somehow, I fell asleep leaning against the wall at the top of the stairs.

I don't know what time it was when suddenly I felt someone holding me close, stroking my hair. I heard Mum's voice, this time warm and soft. 'It's OK, Chee Seng, it will be all right. I promise you. We're going to be all right.'

Chapter 5   *Sons and mothers*

I must have slept well because I woke feeling rested and ready to face the world again. Mum's words had given me new hope. I knew it would be a difficult day because I had to go to school and pretend that everything was normal. But it wasn't normal at all!

Somehow I got through the day. At school, I usually hung out with Dev, Faisal and Ka Choon during the breaks between classes. But that day I managed to avoid them. I knew they would ask all the usual questions about what I'd done at the weekend and stuff like that. How could I answer? I stayed out of their way that first day, and found a quiet corner in the library where no one would disturb me.

When I came out of school I was surprised to see Mum's car. She was waiting to take me home. Amazing! Normally, she never did that. I always took the school bus. On the way home she took me to the ice cream shop. That was something else she never usually did. And when we got home, she insisted on cooking my supper herself. Puri looked at me a bit strangely but she didn't say anything.

After supper, Mum came to my room and checked through my schoolwork. That was something Dad had always done. I felt a bit embarrassed by all the attention but I didn't say anything. I guessed she was trying to make me feel good; trying to make things seem normal.

In fact, it made me feel worse. Things were not normal. Dad was gone. And I didn't really understand why he preferred Auntie Veena to Mum. He'd left Mum but he'd also left me. That was hard for me to accept. He'd turned his back on me and I felt miserable and rejected.

I went to bed early but sleep wouldn't come. Every time I closed my eyes, my mind would start to replay the terrible scene in the bedroom. I kept turning from side to side. I was so tired from everything that had happened and my body was desperate for sleep, but my mind was still wide awake. It wouldn't release me.

I fell asleep at last, but it wasn't a restful sleep. I had lots of bad dreams. In one of them, I was on the sofa watching TV. Raj was lying beside me. Suddenly, he jumped on me. He looked like a devil, his eyes on fire and his teeth bared in a terrible growl. Then his face changed into my father's face. My father, in the shape of a dog, began to tear at my throat. I couldn't breathe ... I was in a panic. I woke up in a sweat.

I slept again, but uneasily. This time, Auntie Veena came towards me wearing a long white dress. She looked so beautiful. She smiled at me and reached out to take me in her arms. But then I saw a big, black, poisonous snake uncurling itself from inside her dress. I ran away but the snake was getting closer and closer to me until ... I woke up again, trembling and sweating.

I went down to the kitchen and took a pot of ice cream from the fridge. I stuffed myself till the pot was empty. Then I went back to bed. I left my bedside light on and somehow I fell asleep again.

* * *

The days and weeks after Dad left us are only a vague memory now. Things settled down somehow but not into a regular, reliable pattern like before. Some days, Mum would be all loving and caring. Other days, she'd shut herself in her room all day or start shouting at me, and even at Puri, for no reason.

As for me, I pretended I was living normally, but inside I felt sick and frightened most of the time. The nightmares got worse. So did the sleeplessness. And I started to eat completely chaotically. Some days I would leave Puri's meals untouched, or I would just pick at them, only eating a few mouthfuls. She never blamed me or complained, but I know she must have been hurt. After all, her meals were always tasty, and she took a lot of trouble to cook all my favourite dishes. But then I would sometimes stuff myself with anything I could find in the kitchen – potato crisps, peanuts, chocolate, ice cream, biscuits, leftovers from supper – anything. Usually, I did this at night when I couldn't sleep. People talk about 'comfort eating', and I certainly felt better after I'd stuffed myself, but the good feeling didn't last. Sometimes I would feel sick after everything I'd eaten. Other times I just felt disgusted with myself. Most days, I'd get up in the morning and leave my breakfast untouched. Not the best way to start the day!

As I said before, as time went by, Mum's moods became more and more unpredictable, and so did her behaviour. Some days she'd be waiting for me outside the school gates, which frankly became embarrassing for me – after all, what sixteen-year-old likes to be treated like a child, especially in front of his friends? On other days, she would forget about me entirely!

When I reached home I got into the habit of just switching on the TV, or playing video games before I did my homework. Gradually, I spent more and more time doing that, and sometimes I didn't do my homework at all.

One day, I came home to find Mum waiting for me. I could see from her face that something was wrong. 'What's going on at school?' she asked accusingly.

'What do you mean?' I replied innocently, trying desperately to work out what was behind her question.

'I've had your class teacher on the phone for the last half-hour. He says your work is terrible. Your grades have gone right down. You haven't been giving in your homework. He even hinted that you might have been copying work from one of your classmates. What's going on?'

'Nothing,' I mumbled. Trust old Mr Chang to go to her behind my back!

'What do you mean "nothing"? You got straight "A"s last term and now you're getting "D"s, when you take the trouble to do anything at all. That's not nothing! You've got your final exams coming up in a few months' time. You can't afford to fail them, you know. That would really be nothing. And you'd be a nothing too. And a nobody. You're old enough to take responsibility for yourself now. Don't expect me to run around after you, checking up on you all the time. I've got plenty of other things to think about.'

I wanted to tell her that I had plenty of other things to think about too, but I knew she'd go wild if I said that. Why were we both pretending that it had nothing to do with Dad? How could she expect me to concentrate when all I could think about was Dad and what he had done? I was trying to make sense of my world – a world that had turned upside down. I wished I could at least talk to him but I knew she'd go crazy if I did that. He had become a 'nobody', just like me. He wasn't supposed to exist at all.

If only she knew the truth about school. Some days, I felt so tired after a sleepless night or a night full of bad dreams, that I would fall asleep in class. Other days, I would sit day-dreaming while the teachers talked on and on about physics or chemistry or history.

I don't know what I would have done without Dev and Faisal and Ka Choon. It was easy to meet up with Dev after school because he lived just up the street. His dad was some sort of accountant in a big law firm in the city. I liked his dad. He was a big man, who never seemed to worry about anything. He was always laughing and joking. Dev's mum made the most delicious *samosas* I'd ever tasted. Dev was tall and thin and told the funniest jokes ever. I think he must have got them from his dad. He was a great hockey-player too. He even played for the Selangor State junior team.

Faisal was a neighbour too. His mum was quite strict with him. As a Muslim, he had to be back for his evening prayers, so sometimes he couldn't join us for our games. He was really good at drawing and painting. I especially loved the cartoons he drew of our teachers! Sometimes we went round to his place to do our homework together – that is, when I did any homework! His mum was a widow. Maybe that's why she was so strict with him, but she was nice too. Anyway, it always felt very friendly round at Faisal's.

Ka Choon was quite different. He was short and fat with thick glasses. His dad was a very wealthy businessman in the building industry, and they lived in a really expensive housing development in Mont Kiara. They had a fantastic apartment with a big terrace, and had the use of all the club facilities like the swimming pool, fitness centre and games room. But Ka Choon's biggest interest was computers.

He was a real expert when it came to the latest programs. He was really good at maths too – a mathematical champion. He used to help me out sometimes. It was as if his brain was some sort of computer – all you had to do was put in the problem, and the answer came straight out. I used to go to his place and sleep over sometimes, but after Dad left us, Mum wouldn't let me out of her sight.

It's funny really that we got on so well. We could hardly have been more different from each other. Dev; tall and athletic, dark-skinned and always joking. Faisal; quiet and serious, and into art in a big way. Ka Choon; short and fat, with his moon face and serious glasses, his mind like a maths calculator. And me, an average-looking Malaysian boy with a talent for writing poems – at least that's what Miss Kumar, our English teacher, said. But we really did get along very well together. They were a great support for me in those first weeks after Dad had gone. I remember telling them about it in the end. I couldn't keep it bottled up inside me any longer. And there was no one else I could talk to.

It was about a month after Dad left and we were sitting up on the playing field after school. I must have been looking miserable because Ka Choon suddenly asked, 'Hey, man, what's up with you? You look as if you've lost a year's allowance. Cheer up!'

'There's something I need to tell you,' I said without thinking. 'Dad has run away with Mum's best friend, and I…' I felt so miserable I couldn't go on. There was a long embarrassed silence. I guess they didn't know how to react.

Dev was the first to speak. He put his arm round my shoulder and gave me a hug. 'Oh, man! I'm so sorry. I knew something was wrong. You've been looking so bad, but … What can we do? Is there anything we can do to help?'

'Not really,' I replied. I felt the tears starting inside me but I forced myself not to cry.

Faisal was really understanding. Maybe it's because he'd lost his own father. 'I know what it's like, Chee Seng. When my dad died, I thought it was the end of the world, but it wasn't. As time goes by, it gets easier, even if you never forget. It's tough but you'll survive. Just hang in there.'

Ka Choon looked uncomfortable and kept taking off his glasses and polishing them nervously. Finally, he spoke. 'I guess every family has something. My dad hasn't run away, but he has two "minor" wives. I know Mum doesn't like it but we pretend all the time that nothing's wrong. But I'm so sorry, Chee Seng. I really am.'

'Come on, guys, let's go back to my place,' Dev broke in. 'Mum will make us some Punjabi[15] snacks to cheer us all up. I think we all need it. And don't forget, let's all agree – this stays between us, right? No gossip at school, OK?'

* * *

After the incident about my school grades, Mum seemed to be always looking for something to complain about. Often, it would be, 'Have you finished your schoolwork? Don't forget what I told you.' Other times, she'd be after me about my meals. 'What sort of rubbish are you eating now? Why don't you wait till Puri cooks you some proper food?' Or 'I told you not to drink so much cola. It's got too much sugar in it. Have some orange juice; it's better for you.'

Often she'd complain about me not tidying my room. 'How many times do I have to tell you to pick your clothes up from the floor? You can't expect Puri to wait on you hand and foot, you know.'

But most of all, she went on and on about Raj. Somehow, all her bottled-up anger seemed to be concentrated on my poor dog. 'Keep that dog off the sofa. There are dog hairs everywhere. And anyway, he makes the house smell bad.' Or 'I don't want to see that dog on your bed again. He'll bring some terrible disease into the house.'

And so it went on, day in, day out, until I was sick of the sound of her voice. Sometimes, I thought she was going insane, especially when she looked at me in that weird way, with her eyes rolling and her hands waving about like the branches of a tree in a storm.

Things came to a head a few months after Dad left. I was missing Dad more and more. He hadn't even called me and there were so many things I wanted to ask him. So many things I wanted him to tell me. Even if it hurt me, I wanted to know.

I had this dream that came back again and again. In my dream, I was standing on a street corner. Traffic was streaming past me. No one would stop for me. Then I saw Dad in a big red sports car. He waved to me and slowed down. I thought he was going to stop but, as I ran to get in the car, he drove away from me. Then he slowed down again. I tried to catch him up but he drove away again. Then, suddenly, there were no other cars, just Dad's. He looked round at me, waved, and drove away in a cloud of dust, like in an American film.

In the end, I felt so bad that I knew I had to speak to him. I waited till I was alone in the house. Mum was at Auntie Swee Eng's and Puri was at the market. I used my mobile and called Dad's number. No reply. I tried his office number but I only got a secretary.

'Hello, can I help you?'

'Can I speak to Mr Yeo? Mr Sammy Yeo?' I replied.

'He's in a meeting,' she explained. 'Who's calling please?'

'This is his … oh, never mind …' I put the phone down. I wanted to talk to him, not his secretary. I tried his mobile again. Still there was no reply. I gave up.

Later, after Mum got back, we were having tea and snacks in the kitchen when my mobile rang. Without thinking, I answered it.

'Hello, Chee Seng? It's me, Dad. You called me. How are you?' His voice sounded tense and unnatural.

'Um, oh … I … er, can I call you back?' I mumbled awkwardly. Mum must have noticed immediately that my voice sounded odd.

'Who's that?' she demanded. Then, seeing my guilty reaction, she grabbed the phone from me. Dad was trying to say something but she screamed, 'Leave my son alone! He doesn't need you. Stay out of our lives.' Then she switched off the phone, threw it onto the table and stormed out.

Chapter 6   *Trying to cope*

Because of the incident with the telephone, Mum got more and more watchful and suspicious of everything I did. Every day we played a game of cat and mouse. I would try to get away with as much as I could, and she would try to catch me out.

'Why do you leave your computer on the whole time?' she asked me one day.

'Why not?' I replied, without thinking.

'Don't you start answering me back all the time,' she complained. 'I have to pay the electricity bills around here. And I notice you never turn off the lights either. You leave the TV on even when you're in your own room. I can't stand all this waste.' I mumbled some sort of apology and started to go back to my room.

'Hey! I haven't finished with you yet!' It was really aggressive, the way she spoke to me, getting worse every day. It made me feel angry and defensive, and I was finding it hard to hide how I felt.

'When do you intend to do your homework, by the way?'

'I'll do it when I'm ready,' I replied.

'You'll do it when I say so!' She was getting really angry.

'No, I won't,' I said. 'Don't keep telling me what to do and when to do it. I'm not a child, you know.'

'Well stop acting like one, then! All you do is lounge about in front of the TV all day, and when you're not there, you're on your computer doing goodness knows what ...'

'What's wrong with that?' I challenged her.

'You need to get some exercise,' she complained. That was a new one. She'd never liked it when I'd gone to the park with Dad. And she never took any exercise herself either!

After that, I made a point of going for long walks with Raj. We would hang out with Dev and some of the other kids, kick a football around, sit around chatting. Then I'd take Raj with me all around the small *lorong*s[16] near our house. It gets dark around 6 pm, and sometimes it happens quite suddenly. One minute it's light, and the next minute the sun has gone and dark clouds cover the sky. I usually got home by six but one day I kept wandering the streets till long after seven. I could hear thunder, and occasional flashes of lightning violently lit up the sky. The palm trees in the gardens were tossing their heads in the wind. Soon the rain would come pouring down. It was already dark when I got home and Mum was waiting for me at the front door, hands on hips and a dark frown on her face.

'What time is this to come home?' she shouted. 'Your supper's been ready for the last hour, and you haven't even thought about your homework. I don't understand you – always running about the streets with that dog.'

'I thought you said you wanted me to get more exercise.' I replied, feeling the now-familiar anger rise inside me.

'Don't answer me back!' she said. 'Get inside right now. Have your supper and start your homework.'

That's more or less the way it was every day, with her finding things to criticise, and me getting angrier and more rebellious every time. I hated the way she spoke about Raj. She should have known how much I cared about that lovely dog, but all she did was complain about him the whole time.

It was a relief when finally Mum got a job. I was upstairs one evening when the phone rang. As usual, I tried to listen in when I heard Mum talking to Auntie Swee Eng. That's how I found out.

'Yes, they called me this afternoon, Swee Eng. I got it! Thanks for putting a word in for me.' There was a pause. 'No, I'm sure it made all the difference,' she continued. 'Sorry? When do I start? Next Monday. They seem to be in a hurry.' Another pause followed. 'What was that? Oh, the pay's not so good to start with, but they said they'll review it after a month's trial.'

It was only later that evening that she actually told me about it. 'Chee Seng, I've decided to go back to work. The money your father gives us to live on is just not enough. So I'm starting a job on Monday.'

'That's great, Mum,' I said, and I meant it. It would be good for her, and even better for me! It would give her something else to think about instead of criticising me all day long. 'What sort of job is it?'

'Oh, it's assistant to an advertising executive in Maha Projections,' she explained. 'It sounds quite challenging, but I already know something about the advertising business. Or at least I did before I married your father, and gave up my job to become a full-time housewife!'

I thought it was time to change the subject, so I just said, 'Good luck, Mum. I bet you'll be a big success.' I meant that too, actually. Mum was a very efficient woman, and I knew she'd get on really well. But of course, I was secretly pleased that I'd now be left on my own, without her constantly complaining about me or Raj.

But life never works out quite as you think it will. I imagined being on my own with Raj, with Puri there to take care of my meals and everything. Things took a different turn the weekend after Mum started work. I overheard her talking to Puri in the kitchen. 'But how will we manage, Puri? You know I'm out all the time now. I need someone here in the house to take care of things. And Chee Seng needs someone to take care of his meals now that I'm not around.'

'Madam, I tell you, is not for long,' Puri explained. 'But my sister, she say my kids in trouble. Is like I tell you, my mama get sick. Need medicine, maybe operation. Cannot take care of kids now.'

'But can't you ask your sister to take care of the problem?' Mum asked.

'She also got her problem, Madam. Her husband run away with some younger girl. You know is like this back home. I have to go, Madam. I stay maybe two, three weeks only. I beg you …'

'But how am I going to manage? I can't take time off from work now; I only just started,' Mum replied.

'Madam, maybe my friend can come sometimes?'

'Your friend?'

'Yes, Madam. You know my friend, Henny? Is Indonesia one. Maybe she come sometimes for help you out?'

'I don't think that will work, Puri. I don't need someone to help out; I need someone here all the time to look after the house.' Mum replied.

In the end, Mum had to let Puri go. I can still see her now in my mind's eye, a small figure holding just one small bag, waving to us as she got into the taxi. Somehow, Mum managed to get a temporary replacement maid from the agency. Her name was Esther, and she was from Indonesia, like Henny. But I didn't like her a bit. Her cooking wasn't tasty like Puri's and she was always on the phone to her friends. We didn't talk much, not like with Puri, but at least she left me alone.

*　*　*

Because Mum wasn't around much, I spent more time with Dev, Faisal and Ka Choon. Mum seemed to like her new job and her mood improved quite a lot. She was more relaxed. She even trusted me to sleep over at Ka Choon's one Saturday night. And she let me invite Dev over to stay one night too, even though he only lived just up the street. Life seemed to be getting better again. Of course, nothing lasts though, does it? Sometimes I think it's just as well that we can't see the future. It would be too depressing.

Anyway, Mum being out a lot meant I spent even more time with Raj too. It's funny the way Raj and me got on together from that very first day when Dad gave him to me. Raj had lovely dark liquid eyes, so full of expression. I know sometimes people laugh when I say this, but I could swear Raj knew what I was thinking before I said anything. He would turn his head to one side and look at me with those eyes full of expression as if to say: 'It's time for us to play football, isn't it?' or 'Shall we go and see Dev now?' or 'How about my supper? You haven't forgotten it, have you?'. If only he could have talked!

He wasn't a very big dog, and goodness knows who his parents were! He was black with white spots. Or maybe he was white with black spots. It was hard to know which! He was perfect for me. His coat wasn't too long and was always very glossy because I used to brush him every day. People always admired him in the street because of his lovely shiny coat.

Every afternoon when I came back from school, Raj and I would run up to the park at the top of the road to meet up with Dev and the others. It had become a routine now that Dad was gone and Mum didn't get back from work till late. But one day, none of my friends were there. I guessed maybe they'd gone to the proper playing field on the other side of the highway. So I set off with Raj to join them.

Now five o'clock in the afternoon was a bad time for traffic in Subang Jaya. There was a main road joining the Federal Highway[17] and the road to the airport, full of cars as people tried to beat the rush hour and get home.

On one side was the leafy old suburb where we lived. On the other was USJ, the newer suburb, with bigger, more modern houses. And that's where the playing field was. There were two lanes on the main road, separated by a division planted with bougainvillea with its purple and orange flowers. I wondered how the plants survived the pollution from the cars, trucks and motorbikes. There were traffic lights here and there and some footbridges for pedestrians, but a lot of people just ran across to save time. When we came to the road, I took one look and decided we'd better not risk it. I walked with Raj to the nearest footbridge and crossed that way.

As I had thought, Dev and the others were playing football. Raj ran ahead of me to join them, barking and running around. He loved to jump in and steal the ball, and the kids didn't seem to mind much. We played for about an hour till it started to get dark, then we all set off back to our own neighbourhood on the other side of the main road.

I don't know why but I just followed the rest of them, instead of using the bridge again. Dev went first. We stood waiting for a gap in the traffic so we could cross the first lane safely. We all made it across just before the stream of traffic started to speed up again. Now we were on the narrow middle division between the two lanes. The traffic was coming from our left and it seemed endless. Cars, taxis, motorbikes, trucks – a stream of vehicles as far as the eye could see. I couldn't see any way we could get across. But now we couldn't go back either. We were trapped in the middle. I wished we had taken the footbridge.

I was holding Raj's collar, when suddenly there was a small gap in the traffic and Dev ran quickly across to the other side. I hesitated, and then it was too late. Dev waved to us to hurry. Before I could stop him, Raj had pulled away from me and rushed across the road towards Dev. But he was too slow. A speeding taxi hit him. He bounced once on the road and landed like a bag of old clothes at the side of the road. The traffic suddenly slowed and I was able to run across to him. A stream of blood was running out of his mouth, and his lovely eyes were expressionless. He moaned once, and died in my arms, there at the side of the road.

Chapter 7 *A new friend*

I know it was stupid, but somehow I blamed Dev for what had happened to Raj. Why had he run across the road before us? If he hadn't waved to us, Raj might have still been alive. I felt so angry. Of course, I was just as much to blame as he was. Why hadn't I used the footbridge? Why hadn't I held on to Raj properly to stop him running out into the road? But, although part of my mind knew it was really my fault, I still blamed Dev. He was terribly upset too, of course, but it was too late. After that, I stopped seeing him. I couldn't face playing football with the memory of Raj always in my mind. I stayed at home instead.

The news about Dad leaving us got around eventually, of course. It always does, I suppose. People are attracted to other people's misfortunes like insects to a candle flame. I don't mean they always enjoy the bad things that happen to other people, but they are certainly fascinated by them. Bad news spreads like a bad smell. Someone smells misfortune in one corner, and before you know it, the world is full of it.

Of course, everyone in the neighbourhood knew about it soon enough. You didn't have to be Sherlock Holmes to notice that Dad's car had gone and that he was never around. And the maids' gossip made sure that the news spread all over the neighbourhood anyway. It's not that Puri had betrayed us or anything like that. After all, how could we hide what was so obvious anyway? But maids love to talk to each other about their employers. So it was inevitable that Puri had told Henny, and Henny had told her friend Risti, and Risti had told... so pretty soon everyone knew. But my school was a long way off and no one had been told about my family problem there, except my closest friends.

Yet somehow, the news eventually reached school too. That was more surprising, to me at least. I couldn't work out how my bad news had got around the school but it had. I couldn't believe Dev or Ka Choon or Faisal would have given me away like that, but who else was there? I noticed them standing together one day, whispering and glancing at me nervously from time to time. They were obviously talking about me. Maybe it was my imagination, but I thought I noticed some of the other kids in the class looking at me a bit strangely too. I thought I could read pity in some of their looks, and a sort of superiority in others. I hated both. I didn't want anyone to pity me, and I certainly didn't want anyone to look down on me.

I started to avoid my friends. In my mind, I was convinced that they were the ones who had spread the story about me. I didn't trust them any more. I felt more and more that I was on my own. There was no one I could rely on any longer. It wasn't a good feeling, yet I felt almost pleasure in my self-pity at being victimised and isolated. It was ridiculous, of course, but it gave me a feeling of something like heroism to be all alone, with the whole world against me – Dad, Mum, my so-called friends, my teachers – everyone. And then, on top of everything else, there was no Puri to look after me, and no Raj to keep me company in my misery. It was a pathetic state of mind to be in, but it seemed quite logical and justified at the time.

*　*　*

Of course, no one said anything to me at first. It was just their looks that told me that they knew. Then one day, something happened to change all that.

It was one of those days in the monsoon season, when the dark clouds would build up as purple as a *mangosteen*[18], and suddenly the skies would open and the rain would fall like someone emptying a lake in the sky. School had just finished but old Mr Chang, our class teacher, had kept me back for some reason. By the time I came out, the school bus had gone. I had no money for a taxi, and there were never any taxis free in weather like that anyway. I was stuck in the pouring rain. I stood in the main doorway of the school feeling lost. Mum was at work so I couldn't call her to pick me up.

Just when I was losing all hope, Ka Ting came through the door and spoke to me. 'Do you need a ride? My dad's driver will be here in a minute. I can drop you home if you like.'

It was a really good piece of luck. And totally unexpected! I knew Ka Ting slightly because he was in the same class, but I'd never had much to do with him. In fact, a lot of the kids avoided him. He was from a very rich family. His father owned all sorts of factories and hotels, and he lived in the really upmarket suburb of UK Heights. The rest of us didn't like him much, or his friend Chee Lick. There were all sorts of rumours about them – problems with girls and drink and stuff like that. But anyway, it was really nice of him to offer to drop me home, so I accepted. There wasn't much else I could have done in the circumstances. It was far better to ride home in a car with him than to stand there in the rain.

'That would be really great,' I replied, 'but I don't think it's on your way. I live in Subang Jaya.'

'Don't worry about it. I'm not in a hurry, and the driver has to go wherever I tell him anyway. Here he comes now. Let's go.'

A shiny white car had just pulled up in front of the door. The uniformed driver, complete with cap and gloves, jumped out of the car and opened the back door for us. I got in without another thought.

'Just tell him your address and relax,' said Ka Ting. I must say that I was quite impressed with the confident way he acted with the driver, whose name was Bala.

It took us quite a time to negotiate the heavy traffic. Bala was a skilful driver, but even he couldn't do the impossible. It was still raining heavily. We moved slowly forward, stopping and starting, overtaking trucks and buses, taking shortcuts wherever there was a complete traffic jam.

'Sorry to hear about your dad,' Ka Ting said. 'It's tough luck.' Obviously he knew too and I was angry for a moment. Then I thought that it was hardly his fault if he knew what everyone else knew too.

'Thanks,' I replied stiffly. 'It's OK now. We can manage.'

'Maybe life's not so much fun though? I mean, what do you do in your spare time?' I'd never really thought about the idea of spare time. Till then, time was time. I went to school. I hung out with my friends – till recently anyway. I stayed at home and watched TV and played video games.

'I don't have that much spare time,' I said, 'what with schoolwork and my mum, and everything…' It sounded pretty pathetic, I knew, but it was true.

'How about parties? Don't you ever go to parties?' he asked.

'Of course I do,' I lied. I hadn't been to many teenage parties, and I felt pretty sure they were not at all like the parties Ka Ting had in mind.

'I mean real parties. You know, when you go out on the town, go to a disco, then go back to someone's house, go wild for the night … Don't you ever go to that kind of party?'

'Um, well, sometimes,' I said, hesitatingly, 'but not very often.' I knew it sounded sort of stupid but I couldn't think of anything better to say.

'Man, you should start to live. I mean really live. Do you have a girlfriend?'

'Um, no, not really … I've never, I mean, it's never happened that …' I was tongue-tied again.

'Wow, man. That's not cool at all. You need a girlfriend to have some real fun. Know what I mean?' He looked at me knowingly, and grinned. 'I mean real fun, OK?'

'Yes, well, I don't know how … I mean, I don't have anyone I like that much.'

'You don't have to marry them, you know. Just have some fun. How about Jessica? Now she's really special. I think she likes you, you know. That's what Wendy told me anyway. She thinks you look romantic.'

Jessica was a girl in our class. She was really pretty, but I'd never thought she would be interested in someone like me. It was a funny feeling to realise that maybe, just maybe, she might think of me in that way. Could I have a chance with her? I didn't want to ask Ka Ting any more about her. Anyway, I was starting to feel a bit uncomfortable with the direction our conversation was taking. Ka Ting went on with all sorts of hints and suggestive comments about girls and getting high and stuff like that. I was relieved when we arrived outside my house.

'Thanks a lot, Ka Ting. See you tomorrow.'

'OK,' he replied, 'and don't forget we must fix a party date soon, right? How about next Saturday?'

'Yeah, maybe. I'll check it out,' I said vaguely, as the car sped off into the rain.

* * *

I noticed Auntie Swee Eng's car in our drive as I ran in to the house. She was sitting in the lounge with a large glass of beer in front of her!

'Hello, Chee Seng.' She turned towards me with a bright smile. 'Your mum called to say she'd be in late tonight. They have some sort of special event at work and she asked me to come over till she gets back. I hope that's all right.' She must have noticed me looking at the beer. 'Oh, sorry,' she said. 'I was really hot and your mum told me to help myself, so I did! There's nothing like a nice glass of cold beer when you feel really thirsty.'

I smiled. There was something faintly odd about this respectable little old woman with a mug of beer. Maybe she could read my thoughts, because she said, 'You mustn't always worry about what people think of you, you know. I'm old enough now to do what I like, when I like, and to hell with what anyone thinks – or says for that matter! Anyway, how are you, Chee Seng? I hope things are a bit better now.'

I didn't quite know what to say. Why would things be better? Dad was gone. My dog was dead. Mum was still acting half-crazy sometimes. My school friends had betrayed me. And there was no Puri to look after me. Better? Again, it was as if she could read my mind.

'Listen, Chee Seng. It may seem that things are not getting any better for you. I know you're still upset about your dad.

And I heard about your dog, Raj. That was a terrible thing to happen. I felt so sad, such a lovely dog. And I know Mum is sometimes a bit hard on you. But try to understand her too. She's going through a really bad time herself. She loves you so much, you know. Never forget that. I don't know what'll happen exactly, but I have a good feeling about you and your mum. You're going to be fine. And don't forget, I'm there too, if you need me. Any time. Now, let's have something to eat, shall we? I brought over some *asam laksa* for that girl to heat up for us. I hope she at least knows how to cook noodles!'

Chapter 8   *Party time*

During the break at school next day, I noticed Ka Ting with his friend Chee Lick talking excitedly to Jessica and Wendy. Wendy was obviously Ka Ting's girlfriend from the way she looked at him. Jessica kept glancing at me. Was it really possible that she was interested in me?

Now I look back on it, I guess I was incredibly innocent for my age. I mean, all the books about teenage boys say how their minds are completely full of sex. But I can honestly say I never thought about sex all that much. Well maybe I did, but it wasn't tied to someone real. It was all in the imagination. Of course, when boys get together, they talk a lot about it, but I think most of it is just talk. It's all about wanting to impress your friends with how adult you are, how much you know and how far you've gone with your girlfriend. That sort of thing. I knew about all the technical stuff – how babies were made and all that – but it all seemed very vague and unconnected to me. I mean, of course I'd wondered what it would be like when it happened, but nothing definite. Things were changing for me though. First of all, I'd seen Dad with Veena, which had certainly shaken up my awareness of sex. And now, I had to admit that I felt that Jessica was really something special, and that maybe …

She was tall like me but the most impressive things about her were her hair (jet-black and hanging almost to her waist), her figure and her eyes. Her eyes were classic

Chinese eyes that sparkled when she smiled. And now she was smiling – smiling at me! She stopped me on the way out of school that afternoon and turned her amazing smile on me. I felt as if the world had suddenly stopped turning...

'Wendy says you might come on Saturday,' she said. 'I hope you can. We're all going to Pop Inn for the disco and then back to my place. It's my seventeenth birthday. Please come. I'd really love you to.' She smiled again and walked away. I couldn't take my eyes off her.

Somehow, I managed to talk Mum into letting me go to the party. 'But I want you home by midnight,' she said, 'and I want to know where you're going. Make sure you give me their telephone number. I don't want you running about the city on a Saturday night. You hear me?'

* * *

Pop Inn was over in Bangsar in a street full of restaurants and bars and discos. Bangsar is one of the centres of nightlife in Kuala Lumpur. It's always bursting with life, especially at night. Foreigners like to go there too so there's always an interesting crowd. We'd arranged to meet outside Pop Inn at eight thirty but I was there early. I felt so nervous and excited. I was looking into a shop window when I felt a hand touch my arm. It was Jessica.

'You're early,' she said. 'That's nice. Let's go for a coffee before the others arrive.'

We found a table in a nearby coffee bar and sat with our drinks. I think she was almost as nervous as me but she didn't show it. 'How does it feel to be seventeen?' I asked.

'I'll tell you that later,' she said. 'I was born at two in the morning. You can ask me again then.' I didn't dare tell her I would have to be home by twelve.

'Oh, I brought you a card, and a small present.' I gave her the card, and the box with the thin silver necklace I'd bought the day before down in Pasar Seni, the old covered market in Chinatown.

'Oh, it's lovely,' Jessica said. 'Can you put it on for me? I want to wear it right now.' She bent her head towards me and I awkwardly fastened the chain around her neck. My hands were trembling, and I could smell her perfume as she shook her long hair back. 'There. How do I look,' she said.

'Like a princess,' I said. It was a pretty silly thing to say, but I honestly did think she looked wonderful.

'Do you really mean that? It's sweet of you. Oh, look, there are the others,' she said. 'Let's go.'

There were six of us – Ka Ting and Wendy, Chee Lick and his girlfriend Ruby, and the two of us. I noticed a sign outside Pop Inn that said 'No admittance for under-18s', but somehow Ka Ting got us all through the door. Inside, the whole place seemed to be shaking to the sound of the music. Bright lights were flashing on and off and we were already in the mood for a party by the time we'd found ourselves a corner table. Ka Ting ordered some drinks from the waitress. Goodness knows what they were, but they tasted fine, sweet and with a strange aftertaste.

'Let's dance,' said Jessica, and there was no way I could refuse, even though I'd never been to a disco before. In fact, you didn't seem to need to know how to dance. The floor was so crowded that it didn't seem to matter what you did. Everyone was just shaking their hips and shoulders and waving their hands in the air. Jessica looked great in her tight T-shirt and short miniskirt. We danced and danced for ages, then went back to our table. The others were still dancing. We were both out of breath. Jessica leant towards me and whispered in my ear.

'Isn't this great? I've wanted to dance with you for such a long time.' Suddenly Jessica kissed me – it was a kiss like I'd never had before. It set my whole body on fire. I felt completely carried away by the music, the dancing and her kiss. I found I was kissing her back, and holding her close to me – things I'd only dreamt of doing with her before.

'Hey! What's all this then?' It was Ka Ting and the others coming back at just the wrong moment. I felt embarrassed and a bit annoyed too. 'There's no hurry, you two. We've got the whole night ahead.' I suddenly came back down to earth. I had to be home by midnight. How could I do that when Jessica obviously had other plans for us?

I glanced at my mobile phone – it was already ten thirty. There was one missed call. Mum was already checking up on me even though it was still ages before midnight. She was behaving like a mother hen with its chick – understandable but irritating. What could I do? I could call her later, and she would insist on me coming straight home. Or I could pretend I hadn't received her call. That wouldn't work with her! Maybe there was another way. What if I asked Jessica's mum to call home for me when we arrived there?

Meantime, Ka Ting was ordering more drinks. He liked to show off like that. The place was bursting with dancers now and the noise was incredible. I could feel the heavy rhythm of the music pumping inside my body like a giant heartbeat. 'Here. Have another drink,' said Ka Ting, 'and try one of these. They'll give you more energy.' He passed around some small white pills. Everyone else seemed happy to take them, so I swallowed mine too. I didn't want to look silly in front of these cool new friends. Jessica took my hand again.

'Come on. Let's dance some more.' How could I resist? This time the DJ had put on a slow record. I took Jessica in my arms, and felt her pressing against me as we danced. It was like a dream. She whispered again in my ear, 'I feel so good with you …'

'Me too …' I murmured. We danced for what seemed like hours, then walked back to the table.

I started to feel really good. The lights suddenly shone brighter and the music was even better. I felt slightly dizzy and light-headed, but everything and everyone seemed to be perfect. I'd never felt so good before. And with Jessica beside me, holding my hand, I felt like a king. The whole world was floating like a brightly coloured dream. I felt as if I could do anything I wanted and I would succeed. I was in heaven …

The next thing I remembered was getting into Ka Ting's big white car and driving away. It was a tight fit for the six of us, but I didn't complain when Jessica had to sit on my knees. My impression of the journey was a succession of flashing lights from the street, and kisses with Jessica. I felt as if I was walking on air when we got out in front of a big house in Ampang. 'Here we are,' she said. 'Welcome to my place.'

We all went inside. I'd never seen a house as big as this one. Not even Ka Choon's. It was magnificent. But then I started to panic. The time. It was already twelve thirty! Mum would be getting very angry.

As I stood there wondering what to do, Jessica took me by the hand and introduced me to a woman who looked a lot like her. Not her mother, surely? She was far too young. 'This is my sister, Jane,' she said. 'She's responsible for everything till tomorrow. My parents have gone to Penang for the weekend. They're not here much anyway, so Jane's the one who's responsible most of the time.'

'Hi,' said Jane, with a warm smile. 'You're Chee Seng, right? I had a call from a lady a little while ago. She seemed a bit anxious about you. I told her you'd be here soon and not to worry. Maybe you should call her.'

I went to a side room and dialled our home number. But the person who picked up the phone was not Mum. For a moment I was confused, then I recognised Auntie Swee Eng's voice. 'Hello, Chee Seng,' she said. 'I've been worrying about you. Your mum said you were due back by midnight.'

'But where's Mum,' I asked, suddenly feeling worried. 'What's going on? Why isn't she there? Has something happened?' My mind was still spinning from all the excitement of the evening, but I suddenly felt a cold finger of fear down the back of my neck.

'Nothing for you to worry about,' said Auntie Swee Eng, in a reassuring voice. 'She had to leave for Melaka unexpectedly. Your Aunt Mei Ling is in hospital again. Mum will be back tomorrow evening. She asked me to take over. I think you're in luck!' I could picture her smiling as she said that. 'Now, I know you should be back home by now. But just let me speak to that nice lady again, will you?'

I called Jane from the next room and handed her the phone. She made a sign for me to leave. As I went out, I heard her saying, 'Oh, hello again. No, no trouble. Everything's fine. They're having fun. It's Jessica's birthday so ... No, no.

51

We'll make sure he gets back safely. There's plenty of room here…' A few minutes later she called me and handed me back the phone. 'It's OK,' she whispered.

'Hello? Chee Seng? Now listen to me. Your mother would probably kill me if she ever found out, but that lady sounds fine. And I know you're having fun, so you can stay. You're only young once. They'll send you back in the car tomorrow when you get up. But don't come back too late! Your mum is certain to call me to check on you. So … enjoy yourself. I'm off to bed. Goodnight.'

Was I dreaming? My problem had been solved as if by magic, and the night was still young. I floated back to join the others, my head still spinning, and my feet hardly touching the ground. Jessica's sister Jane had disappeared, leaving us to ourselves.

'OK, guys, let's party,' said Ka Ting. Jessica put on some music, and turned down the lights. 'If anyone needs anything to drink, or snacks, the kitchen's over there,' she said. We all started dancing again, all around the room, and outside on the terrace overlooking the swimming pool.

After a while, Jessica took my hand and whispered, 'Come with me. I want to show you something.' We left the room and she led me upstairs and through a door. It was dark but we didn't need light. She pulled me to her and we started kissing again. 'This is my room,' she murmured. 'Let's make ourselves comfortable, soon I'll be seventeen …' I could hardly believe what was happening, but it was wonderful and I followed Jessica's lead, without any thoughts about where it might take us …

Chapter 9   *Breaking out*

I woke up with a splitting headache. My mouth was as dry as the desert sands. I felt ill, as if I might be sick at any moment. My eyes couldn't focus properly – everything looked unclear and things kept changing their shape – they wouldn't stay still. I didn't recognise the room from the night before. How had I got there? There was no sign of Jessica. I was alone but someone had folded my clothes neatly and put them on a chair by the bed. There was a large glass of water too, which I drank down quickly, though it didn't seem to make me less thirsty.

I almost fell out of bed and made my way unsteadily to the bathroom, my knees as weak as water. Somehow I managed to have a shower, get dressed and make my way downstairs to the kitchen. The clock said eleven. How long had I slept? I didn't know because I still couldn't clearly remember when I'd fallen asleep. Outside it was raining.

I was relieved when Jane came in, looking fresh and cheerful. 'Good morning!' she said brightly. 'I hope you enjoyed the party. Jessica's already gone out for her tennis lesson. She asked me to give you this.'

She passed me a folded sheet of paper. I read it –

Dear Chee Seng,
I hope you slept well. It was great last night. And you were great too! I won't be back till this afternoon. Jane will look

after you. Please call me when you get home – 012-567891.
It's my mobile. I've got so much to say to you, I can hardly
wait. See you tomorrow.
Love,
Jessica.

I couldn't face any breakfast, so Jane drove me back home in her red sports car. It was just like the one Dad had been driving in my dream. We didn't talk much but I felt quite at home with Jane. She was another one of those adults who doesn't make a fuss – just treated you like a normal human being, like Auntie Swee Eng. Just before she dropped me outside the house and drove off, she said, 'I'm glad Jessica seems to like you so much. She needs a good friend. I hope you can come again soon.'

Auntie Swee Eng was waiting for me at the front door. She looked as neat and tidy as always, with her usual warm smile on her face. 'Here comes the party hero,' she joked. 'Now, have you had any breakfast?'

I shook my head. 'I see. Not feeling like eating, is that it? All right, Chee Seng, I think you'd better take a rest for a while. You look as if you need it.' I looked at myself in the hall mirror and I could see what she meant.

I spent the afternoon asleep in my room. There seemed to be something wrong with my mind. I felt as if I was dreaming, but it was more like a weird series of pictures flashing through my head. It was as if I was re-experiencing the events of the previous night and more …

I got up around five in the afternoon, still feeling a bit confused. Auntie Swee Eng was waiting downstairs. Mum was still not back.

'So, you had a good time last night?' she asked. I nodded. 'Good. Well, I don't think we need to go into the details with your mum. But, for the future, just remember that your old Auntie Swee Eng may not always be there to protect you. So, be careful!'

'Thanks,' I said, feeling a bit uncomfortable. 'I'll remember that.'

'When I see you like this,' she said, 'it reminds me of when I was young myself. Maybe I'll tell you about that some day. By the way, a young lady called. Said her name was Jessica. She asked if you were all right.'

I suddenly realised that I had completely forgotten about phoning Jessica. I went to my room and called her number on my mobile. But when I heard her voice, I suddenly felt tongue-tied. I didn't know what to say.

'Hi, Jessica.'

'Hi, Chee Seng. Are you OK? Jane said you looked a bit unwell when she dropped you off today.'

'Erm, I, er, slept a bit. I feel better now. How about you?'

'Oh, I'm fine.' Jessica replied. 'I was a bit sleepy this morning but the tennis helped …' There was a silence, as if neither of us knew what to say next.

'So, erm, I'll see you tomorrow then,' I said, rather obviously.

'Yes, of course. How about next weekend? Will you be free on Saturday again? I think Ka Ting is planning something special.' There was another silence. 'So what do you think, Chee Seng? You know, it was good to be with you last night …'

'Erm, yes. It was good, Jessica. I'll try to get permission from Mum but she's kind of difficult sometimes.' I felt stupid telling her this. It made me feel like a little boy in short trousers! I felt my anger rising against Mum again.

'Oh, I see,' said Jessica in a disappointed voice. 'Well, let me know, OK? So … I guess I'd better say bye for now. I still have some things to do before I go to bed.'

And before I had time to say 'bye' she'd put the phone down. Obviously she thought I was acting like a baby. I'd messed up everything with her. I felt angry with myself … and with Mum. Why hadn't I told Jessica how wonderful she was, how much I'd loved being with her and what we'd done together? But my tongue had turned to wood in my mouth. Now I felt I'd lost her.

The next day when we met in school, Jessica didn't make any special effort to talk to me or be alone with me. She acted quite cold and distant. I felt that I really had lost her. She was too grown up for a kid who had to ask his mum for permission to do the smallest thing.

At least Ka Ting was still very friendly. 'Hey, Chee Seng, that was some party, eh? And I told you Jessica likes you. Now you can see how much, right?' And he grinned. 'I'm having a party at my place next Saturday. You'll come again, won't you? I'll make sure Jessica comes too, don't worry. And we'll have plenty of good stuff like last time. It's going to be really cool. You can sleep over too, so no need to worry about time.'

I thought about being with Jessica again, and then the trouble I would have with Mum. 'Sounds great,' I said. 'I'll let you know, OK?'

'Sure,' he said, and walked over to talk to his friends.

That week I kept on thinking about the party over and over again. How could I get away again? I was sure Mum would refuse to let me go. But I had to see Jessica again, and show her she was wrong about me – show her I really wanted to be with her. The word 'love' kept passing through my mind, but I felt a bit uneasy with that word after what Dad had done to us. Anyway, by Wednesday, I'd made up my mind. I would ask Mum, and, if she refused, I would go to the party anyway!

As I expected, it was not an easy conversation. 'Mum, I was wondering about Saturday …' I began hesitantly.

'Wondering what?' she asked suspiciously, as if she already knew what was coming next.

'Well, er, there's this friend of mine from school, Ka Ting, and he's invited me to a party at his place on Saturday. He says I can sleep over, so no need for you to pick me up …'

'You went to a party last Saturday too. You can't expect to go to parties every weekend, you know. What about your schoolwork? How do you expect to get it all done if you're out at parties all the time? And anyway, who is this Ka Ting? It's the first time you've mentioned him. What do we know about him? What about his family? What sort of people are they? How do I know what you're getting up to at these parties?'

'But it's not fair, Mum,' I protested. 'All the other kids get to go to parties.'

'You're not all the other kids. You're my son. And believe me, I know what's best for you. So, if I say you're not going to the party, you're not going, and that's that!'

I stormed off to my bedroom, boiling with anger at the injustice, the unfairness of it. But now I was determined to go to the party, never mind the consequences.

* * *

The next day, I finally managed to talk to Jessica alone, for the first time that week. 'Jessica, I'm coming on Saturday. I really want to be with you again. I'm sorry about the other day. I was feeling a bit strange, I don't know why.'

'That's OK. I'm glad you can come.' And she smiled at me warmly, the way she had before, and I felt my heart miss a beat. 'How are you getting there?' she asked me. 'Jane will be taking me, so we could pick you up if you like.'

'That would be great,' I said, 'but maybe you could pick me up outside Holiday Stores, not from my place?'

'Fine, why not? Say around eight thirty?'

'Great,' I said. But my mind was racing on, thinking how I was going to get out of the house under the nose of my watchful mother.

*　*　*

The rest of the week seemed to last for ever. I went through the routine of classes, homework and meals as if I was sleepwalking. All I could think of was how to get away on Saturday. Friday night came, and Saturday morning. The moment of truth was almost there. But once again, luck was on my side. Mum had a call from one of her cousins, who was over from the United States, inviting her for dinner. Before she left, she warned me again.

'I want you to finish your homework and have an early night. Don't forget! I'll be back by ten thirty at the latest.' I wished she would stop trying to push me around like that, but I didn't say anything.

As soon as she'd gone, I got ready for the party. I wanted to look my best for Jessica. I put oil on my hair and wore my tightest jeans, with my Italian shoes and an open-necked shirt. Then I left a note for Mum to tell her not to worry. I said I'd call her later. The maid was off duty. I walked up to Holiday Stores shortly before eight thirty.

Right on time the sports car pulled up, with Jane at the wheel and Jessica sitting next to her. Jessica looked great again with her long black hair and a tight green dress. I climbed into the back seat and we drove off.

This time I thought Jane was a bit tense, and the two sisters didn't talk on the way to Ka Ting's. As we got out, she said to Jessica, 'Don't forget what I told you. I'll pick you up soon after midnight. Just call me. You know Mum wants you home tonight. No sleeping over, especially at that Ka Ting's place. You know why. I'm trusting you with her, Chee Seng. Make sure she calls, OK? Don't let me down. Anyway, have a good time, the two of you.'

For a moment she sounded almost like my own mum, and I wondered what she meant by 'that Ka Ting'. But I was so happy to be left with Jessica that I thought no more about it.

The party was even better than the week before. Ka Ting's father was away. In fact, he always seemed to be away, so Ka Ting had the house to himself. And what a house it was! Even bigger than Jessica's, with a huge games room and an enormous swimming pool surrounded by palm trees and flowering bushes and even a fully-equipped gym. There were about thirty people there, some of them quite a bit older than me. The party started on the terrace with some dancing and a few drinks. Again, there were things I'd never tasted before – they were brightly coloured, sweet and left a strange aftertaste in the mouth. Every time I drank one it made me want another. I danced with Jessica, of course, and soon we were sitting together in a dark corner, kissing just like the week before. It was magical. There was a wonderful buffet laid out, and we were soon piling our plates high, Malaysian style. As we sat enjoying our food, Ka Ting came round again.

'How is it, you two? Having a good time, right? But it's time to really party now. Come on. Here's something to give you an extra lift.'

He slipped two of the little white pills into my hand. I remembered how wonderful I'd felt at the disco after taking the pills, but then I thought about how sick I'd felt the next day. I decided that the pills weren't good for me, so I put them in my pocket. But Jessica must have taken hers. Soon she became all dreamy and soft as we began to dance to a slow record just like before. Jessica felt like liquid honey melting in my arms. The time just slipped away but I suddenly remembered what Jane had said. 'Jessica, I think you'd better call Jane. Don't forget what she told you. I don't want to get you into trouble.'

'Oh, Chee Seng. I want to stay here with you. I'm sure Ka Ting won't mind if we sleep over at his place. Come on...' I have to admit I was really tempted, but I insisted that she should call Jane. Jessica really didn't want to but in the end she called her sister, who said she'd be there in half an hour. As soon as she rang off, Jessica grabbed my hand and pulled me into the house. We found a quiet corner to be alone together for the few moments we had left.

As we were leaving, Ka Ting took me aside and whispered, 'There's no need for you to go! We're just starting to have some real fun, you know. Some of those big guys have brought some really special stuff. You should stay on and try it. It'll give you the biggest high you've ever felt. Don't worry, you can stay here till tomorrow. Let Jessica go if you like, but there are plenty of other girls here tonight. Later we'll all get in the pool together, you know... How about it?'

'Sorry, Ka Ting, but I promised Jessica I'd go with her. Maybe another time …'

'That's right,' Ka Ting said in strange, empty-sounding voice. 'That's right, my friend. Anyway, you take these for later. Maybe you can take them tomorrow when you need a pick-me-up.' And he pressed a few of the little white pills into my hand. I put them in my pocket. 'And don't forget, you can always come over here. No problem. Drinks and stuff and plenty of fun, right?'

Jane dropped me off at my gate, and I squeezed Jessica's hand as I got out. When I looked round, the car had already gone, leaving me alone to face the full force of Mum's fury. My hands were sweaty and shaking and I nearly dropped the keys. Sure enough, there she was, waiting for me, like a dragon breathing fire. She looked as if she might explode. It was payback time!

Chapter 10   *Jessica's problem*

'Come here,' Mum said with a voice like ice, 'if you can walk straight!' As I walked unsteadily towards her, I felt that something unthinkable was about to happen. Something that would change us both for ever. And now it was too late to stop it. I had almost reached her when she slapped me hard across the face. And I mean hard! I felt the sting and something wet on my cheek. It was blood where her ring had cut me.

'Let that teach you to make a fool of me,' she said, breathing heavily and trembling. I think she had shocked herself as much as me by the violence of her reaction. 'We'll talk about this in the morning. Now get out of my sight. You make me sick. Sick, sick, sick. After everything I've been through lately, all you can do is make it worse. You're selfish, stupid and you obviously have no feelings – at least no feelings for me. Now get up to your room before I lose my temper again.'

As I undressed and washed, I thought of all the things I wished I'd said to her. Some of them would have hurt her as much as she'd hurt me. But it was too late now. I tried to get to sleep but I couldn't stop thinking about everything – about Jessica, about Mum, about Dad. My head was spinning with questions but no clear answers. I felt confused, angry and unhappy.

* * *

I slept late the next morning. Maybe my mind was unconsciously hoping that Mum would be out. But she was waiting for me when I came downstairs for breakfast. I felt fear deep down in my stomach – that terrible sinking feeling everyone gets when they know something bad is about to happen to them. She followed me to the table and sat down with me, and poured herself a cup of coffee. Her face was tense and her eyes unsmiling. 'So what's going on then?' she asked in a hard, cold voice.

'Nothing,' I mumbled as I tried to swallow some cereal. It tasted like cement.

'Don't think I'm stupid,' she went on. 'I know you've been up to no good, so it's no good pretending and telling me a load of stupid lies. I told you not to go to that party last night but you went anyway. You deliberately did what I told you not to do. I want to know why.'

How could I explain the reasons to her? She would never understand how I felt about Jessica, or how exciting it was to be having fun with my new friends – the drinks and the partying – or how I just needed to get out of the house. I just mumbled some sort of protest. 'I work at school all week and I stay here locked up like a prisoner doing my homework night after night. I'm not allowed to do this, not allowed to do that. You won't let me out of your sight. Why can't I go out at least once a week to enjoy myself a bit and have some fun with my friends? It's not fair.'

'Life isn't fair,' she said roughly, 'as you should know by now. If life was fair, your father would still be here taking proper care of us instead of running around with that woman. So don't you talk to me about what's fair and what isn't.'

'Why do you always bring up Dad?' I said accusingly. 'It's as if you're blaming me for what happened.'

'Don't you dare speak to me like that!' she said. 'He's left me to look after you and I intend to make sure you grow up as a civilised human being. And I couldn't care less whether you think that's fair or not!'

She paused and looked at me hard, her eyes shining dangerously. I pushed my bowl of uneaten cereal away. She started to clear the breakfast things noisily. 'So I'm telling you one last time – if I say you are not to do something, then you'd better not do it. No more parties or going out at all till Puri gets back. That's in a couple of weeks from now.'

'But I thought she was due back this week,' I said.

'She called me last night to say she can't come back for another two weeks. There's nothing I can do about it. Anyway, once she's back, she'll be around to keep an eye on you. Till then, no more going out with your friends, and no allowance either. Do I make myself clear? I've got enough to worry about without having to worry about you, too, all the time. Now I'm going over to see Auntie Swee Eng. Do you want to come?'

'No thanks,' I said. Actually, I would have liked to have seen Auntie Swee Eng – but not now, and certainly not with my mother.

'In that case, you'd better get on with your homework. I'll take a look at it when I get back this evening. There's some food in the fridge for your lunch.'

* * *

Soon after she'd left, I got a text message from Jessica. She must have tried to call while I was arguing with Mum.

Got 2 cu. V imp. Can u call? Luv u, J

I wondered what was so important, so I called her straight away. 'Hi, Jessica.'

'Oh, Chee Seng – thank goodness you've called. I've been going mad. Look, I've got to see you. Something terrible is happening. I don't want to talk about it on the phone. When can I see you?'

I thought fast. I couldn't go out after what Mum had just said. What could I do? I knew I had to see Jessica. She sounded really upset. Why not ask her to come over? Mum would only be back in the evening, and it was the maid's day off. No one would know. 'Listen, Jessica, can you come here to my place? I can't leave the house today. Can you get a taxi or something?'

'Chee Seng, give me a few minutes to work it out. I'll call you back, OK?'

She phoned ten minutes later to say that she'd be there by midday. We didn't speak much, but I could hear the tension in her voice. I knew something really serious was going on. It was already eleven o'clock, so I went to tidy myself up before she arrived. I'd never had a girl over before and I felt pretty nervous about it.

At exactly midday a red and white Comfort taxi stopped outside our gate and Jessica got out. When I let her in the house I could see she'd been crying. Her eyes were red and swollen, and she looked exhausted. I took her in my arms and kissed her gently. Suddenly she began crying uncontrollably. I took her into the lounge and made her comfortable on the big sofa. Then I gave her some water to drink and sat down beside her. Gradually she calmed down and gave me a sad smile as she wiped her tears away. 'So what's wrong?' I asked.

'It's terrible, Chee Seng. They're sending me away.'
'Away where?'

'To Australia. Dad's sister is married to an Australian in Perth, and Mum and Dad have decided to send me there to finish school and go to university.'

'But why? I mean why now?' I asked.

'Don't ask me. I guess it's because they're worried about what's been happening to me. I didn't tell you all this before because I was so happy to be going out with you, but I had a bad experience with a guy I met at Ka Ting's a few months ago. He was married and was just using me for fun. Please don't ask me anything else about it. I was stupid. It was nothing important. I just wanted to forget about it, but my parents found out and now they're always reminding me of it. And then, my Mum found some of those party pills in my bedroom. She went wild. That's when they started to talk about Australia. I didn't believe them at first but this morning they told me it's definite. I have to go, they say. They think if I stay here, I'll get into really deep trouble. They want me out of here and somewhere they think I can't get into trouble.'

'But, if you go to live in Australia …' I began.

'Yes, I know … then I'll never see you again,' she said, and tears began to pour down her cheeks. I took her in my arms and stroked her hair slowly to calm her down.

'When do they want you to go?'

'At the end of this term. That's only two weeks away. What are we going to do? I think I'll die if I have to leave you.'

'Can't you persuade them to change their minds?' I asked, knowing the answer already.

'I've tried. Believe me, I've tried. But they've made up their minds. There's nothing I can do to change that.'

'So, what are we going to do? I need to see you, Jessica. You know that. I can't live without seeing you. I've never felt this way before but …'

'It's the same for me, Chee Seng. That's why I had to talk to you. We have to find a way out of this. Somehow. Any way we can …'

We spent the next few hours together. We shared the food Mum had left in the fridge. We talked about how we felt about each other. We went round and round in circles, trying to find a way out of Jessica's move to Australia, but couldn't find an answer. Eventually, we went to my room. We lay down together …

It was 5 pm by the time Jessica left. We'd agreed to meet after school the next day to see if either of us had thought of a solution.

I tried to concentrate on my homework, but my head was full of thoughts of Jessica. Somehow I managed to finish everything just before Mum came back for dinner. She read through my homework absent-mindedly, as if she had problems to deal with too. I wondered if something had happened at work. She really looked worried.

* * *

The next day, at school, Ka Ting took me to one side during the break. 'Hey man!' he said. 'You should have stayed on Saturday – it got really wild. We all ended up swimming naked in the pool till the sun came up! It was some party. Dad's away in China again next weekend. I'm planning another party on Saturday. It's going to be even better this time. You come, OK? Bring Jessica too, right?'

'Listen, Ka Ting,' I replied. 'I can't go anywhere for a couple of weeks. And what's more, I don't have any money. Mum's cut my allowance. I'm in deep trouble at home.'

'Don't worry!' he said, laughing. 'No need to worry. I can lend you some money. Here.' And he slipped two fifty-ringgit[19] notes into my hand – more than my usual weekly allowance. 'You can give it back later, no problem.'

'But I still can't get away on Saturday. I'm stuck at home. She's watching me like a guard dog.'

'No problem … I'll have another party after that. You just come anytime, OK?'

As he said that, an idea started to form in my mind. Perhaps there was a way out of our problem after all …

Chapter 11 *A way of escape*

I managed to speak to Jessica in a quiet corner of the library before we went home that day. 'Jessica, I have an idea. But first I have to know one thing. Are you sure you really want to be with me? Are you sure you'd do anything not to go to Australia? I have to know because …'

She stretched out her hand and laid a finger on my lips. 'I'm sure. Don't ask me that again, OK?'

'So, listen to my idea and tell me if you think I'm completely crazy …'

Jessica took my hand. 'I'd do anything to be with you, crazy or not.'

'I've been thinking about Ka Ting,' I started to explain, 'I think he could help us to run away together.'

'Run away? But where to? They'd find us, and then it would be worse. Tell me, Chee Seng, where could we go?'

'Just listen. Here's my plan. We go to a party at Ka Ting's place. Not this Saturday, the one after. That's just before you're due to leave for Australia. You can say it's your going-away party. When everyone else is leaving, we pretend to leave too, but then we come back. We stay over at his place for the night, then take a bus up to Perlis. My uncle has a bungalow up there. He hardly ever uses it. I know where he keeps the key. We can stay there for a few days. Then we cross into Thailand. It's easy! I've done it before with my parents. Once we're there, we can find jobs. We both speak good English, so getting a job in a hotel or something won't be a problem. No one will find us.'

'But, Chee Seng, we'll need to prepare everything. We haven't got much time. I'll sort out the things I'll need to take. We'll need money too. Have you got a savings account?'

'Erm, no, I haven't, but I think I know where I can get some money before we leave. Anyway, I'll start sorting out some stuff to take as well. We'll have to travel light, so no big suitcases, right? Just backpacks.'

'And we'll have to work out how to leave home without attracting attention,' added Jessica. Obviously both of us were thinking practically about the details. But I wondered secretly whether our daring plan would work. Perhaps it was crazy. And we would have to tell Ka Ting too.

Every day that followed, Jessica and I would find time to meet and talk about how our preparations were going. It brought us even closer together. Even though I sometimes felt nervous butterflies in my stomach, the excitement of our secret plan made me feel more alive than I'd ever felt before.

At home, things were fairly quiet. I tried to do everything I could to behave normally and do whatever Mum asked me. That way, I thought, I would make her less suspicious, and it might be easier for me to slip away when the time came. I noticed she was looking very stressed and tired again. I wondered if it was something to do with her work but I decided it was better not to ask, in case she got angry again. Being around Mum was like walking on eggshells.

One evening that week, she came home late from work while I was upstairs doing my homework. When I went down, she was sitting at the table with some whisky in front of her. She had her glasses on and was reading through a thick file of papers, absent-mindedly picking at a plate of potato crisps. She looked tired. She was so absorbed in her thoughts that she didn't seem to notice me.

After a few moments, Mum looked up. 'Come and sit down a minute, Chee Seng. I want to talk to you.' I sat down facing her across the table. Now that I could see her properly, I noticed that her eyes were red, and her hands were trembling slightly. She didn't look well. Maybe it was the effect of the whisky – Mum didn't usually drink. I wondered why she was drinking now.

'Listen, Chee Seng. There's something I want to tell you.' Her voice sounded tired and lifeless, and I suddenly felt a wave of love for her. For a moment, I forgot about how hard she'd been on me. 'I'm having some problems at work,' she continued. 'I can't explain it all right now but things aren't going well. I'm not sure how long I can carry on working there. I just want you to know that because, if I have to leave, we'll have trouble paying for everything.'

I didn't know how to reply, but she had more to say. 'I haven't been feeling well lately and I can't sleep properly. Dr Narasiman has given me a lot of pills to take, to help me relax and sleep. He says it may be something to do with stress. I hate taking all that medicine. It makes me feel even worse.'

'I'm sorry, Mum,' I sympathised. 'What can I do? Anything?'

'No, not really. I just wanted you to know, that's all. I know it's not easy for you now, but let's try to get on as well together as we can, right?'

'OK, Mum,' I agreed.

'Oh, and one other thing. Auntie Swee Eng has invited you over for dinner with her on Saturday night. I have to go to Melaka again – Mei Ling is still in hospital. I'll be back late, so it'll be good for you to have some company.'

I was really happy to hear this. I'd agreed with Jessica that we'd both be on our best behaviour till we ran away, to avoid creating suspicion. I hadn't seen Auntie Swee Eng for a while anyway, and I always enjoyed spending time with her.

So that Saturday evening, Auntie Swee Eng came over to pick me up and take me to her place. The moment I saw her, I felt better. That's the effect she always has on me. We sat on the terrace of her small house drinking mango juice and enjoying the cool of her garden. The jasmine flowers were releasing their sweet evening perfume. Life felt good.

'I love this time of day,' she commented with a smile. 'It's as if the world can breathe again after the heat and dust of the day. So how are things with you, Chee Seng?'

'More or less all right,' I replied.

'How's school? Or maybe I shouldn't ask that. You must get fed up with adults asking you about school. As if nothing else was important! I used to hate that question when I was a girl. So what else is going on with you, Chee Seng? You know, I worry about you and your mother a lot. She's having a hard time at the moment. What do you think?'

'I think you're right,' I answered. 'She's got some sort of problem at work, and she told me she's taking a lot of pills for stress and because she can't sleep. I'm worried too.'

'Oh, so that explains it. She's been looking unwell for some time now. I'll talk to her. I think she needs another woman to talk to. As for her work, she did mention some problems to me a while ago. You know, Chee Seng, it's worse than a jungle in some of these companies. People will do anything to get promoted. Thank goodness I'm retired!'

The way she said it made me realise that she'd probably had a similar experience to Mum's. Anyway, I was glad I'd mentioned it. If anyone could help Mum, it was Swee Eng.

We spent a lovely evening together. She'd prepared some delicious *asam laksa*, and some *gula melaka*[20] for dessert. She played me some of her CDs – Mozart and Schumann. I never usually listened to that kind of music, but with her it seemed quite normal, and not like showing off. She loved classical music and showed me what it was like to get deep enjoyment from it. I even started to feel moved by it too.

Later on, Auntie Swee Eng started to tell me a bit about her own life. She got out some old family photograph albums. They were full of pictures – brown with age – of couples getting married, babies, and family photos from many years ago. 'That's your great-grandfather and grandmother,' she said, pointing at a man in a formal black jacket, white shirt with a high collar and black bow tie. He looked very serious. He stood behind his wife. She was wearing traditional Peranakan dress, with small decorated shoes, a long *sarong* and a *kebaya*. Her hair was tied back and she wasn't smiling. It seemed incredible that these had been real people with real lives, and real problems just like us. Looking at the photos with her I started to understand how I was part of this network of roots stretching back. I wondered how my own grandchildren would think of me when I was dead and gone.

Then she opened a page with just one photograph of an incredibly beautiful young woman. I realised with a sudden shock that this was Auntie Swee Eng when she was younger. 'Is that you?' I asked, just to make sure.

'It is. What a change the years make, don't they?' She sighed and turned the page. There was a picture of a handsome Indian man, wearing white shorts and an open-necked shirt, standing between rows of rubber trees and smiling into the camera. In the next picture the same man was standing with Swee Eng. She was wearing a light cotton dress and looking up at him. They were holding hands. They both seemed completely happy.

'Who's that?' I asked. Auntie Swee Eng didn't answer immediately. She seemed to be lost in the photograph, and her eyes were far away.

'That's Gana,' she eventually replied, without moving her eyes from the photograph.

'Where was the picture taken?' I didn't like to ask anything more personal, though I'd have loved to have known more about this man and Auntie Swee Eng.

'That was on the rubber estate in Perak,' she explained. 'Gana was the assistant manager. There was still a British manager even then. It was not long after independence.'

'How did you meet Gana?' I asked.

'Well, in those days, it wasn't easy to meet young men, especially if you came from the sort of background I was brought up in. You know Daddy, that's your Great-uncle Lim, held an important position in the Ministry of Agriculture. He was fairly well-off – though not like some of these new rich around today. I was one of six children. There's only me and your Auntie Rosie left now. We were brought up very strictly. Study, study, study – we were all expected to be top of the class. There was church twice on Sunday. No parties, no dances, and no drinking. We were made to believe that our community was somehow better than others. We were the top of society and expected to prove it by being the best at everything.'

'But when was that?' I asked

'Well, Daddy was doing very well before the war – the Second World War – until the Japanese invasion of Malaya in 1941. That was the year I was born. We had a hard time. I don't know how my parents managed to raise six kids.'

'So what about after the war?'

'Well, Daddy got his job back, and we thought everything would go back to the way it was before, but it didn't. After a while the movement for independence started up. We finally got it in 1957. That was an exciting time. I was just sixteen and preparing for my school leaving exams.'

'Did you pass your exams?' I asked, thinking about my own miserable performance earlier in the year!

'Oh yes. I got distinctions. Everything was planned for me to do my A levels, then go to London to study law.'

'And did you?'

'Did I what? Pass my A levels? Yes. Go to London? No. Something else happened. I went to Singapore instead.' She looked again at the picture of herself with Gana.

'I see.' It was a stupid thing to say.

'You do, do you?' she said, with a sad smile. 'I doubt it. Anyway, after independence things got more difficult for Daddy. They were trying to promote more Malays in the civil service. Nothing wrong with that, of course, but Daddy didn't feel he could stay on. So he retired while I was in my last year at school. But not before I met Gana.'

'How did you meet him?' I asked her.

She sighed. 'Maybe we should leave that for another time. Come on. I'll take you home.'

Chapter 12 *The best plans…*

I felt a bit guilty about using Auntie Swee Eng, but if I went to her house the following Saturday, it would give me the perfect way to get to Ka Ting's later in the evening. My plan was starting to look possible after all. I would go to Auntie Swee Eng's, return home before Mum got back, pick up my things and meet Jessica at Ka Ting's.

On Monday, Jessica and I met to discuss things as usual. She'd also worked out how to get away. She would take her backpack to school on Friday and give it to Ka Ting to take to his place. I spoke to him and asked him if we could stay the night after the party. 'No problem!' he said with a knowing smile. 'Stay as long as you like.'

'But no one else must know, OK?'

'OK, cool.'

I don't know how we got through that week. I could feel myself getting more nervous as each day passed and Saturday approached. And Jessica was showing signs of stress too. We even had a few arguments – nothing serious but we were both on edge. The slightest thing would set us off.

At home, I was careful to behave as normally as possible. I made sure I did my homework on time, and that I was always around when Mum came home. She was still looking very tired and sick. Her face was always tense and her skin was an unhealthy grey colour. She was still taking her medicine but that didn't seem to be helping her much. I was worried about her, but my mind was occupied with Jessica and our plan to run away together. I tried to stay off the topic of Mum's work when we spoke, which wasn't often. But just when things seemed a bit calmer, she started to complain about my schoolwork again and we had another fight. So I didn't feel so bad about leaving, after all.

On Wednesday evening Mum got home later than usual. I came down to sit with her as she had her dinner. I had this strange feeling. Everything felt normal, yet I knew that in just three days I would be leaving her alone, and we would never sit together like this again. It was as if I were two people at the same time – one playing the loving son, and the other the rebel who would desert her. And each of these two people could see the other and was wondering just how they could exist together in the same body.

She asked me about my day. 'So how did you get on?'

'Not bad,' I answered. 'I got an "A" for my English essay, and a "B plus" for my maths project.'

'That's an improvement,' she commented with a sad smile. 'Oh, and by the way, Auntie Swee Eng called to ask me to remind you that you're going over for dinner again on Saturday. It's a real help to me. I'll have to drive down to Melaka again to see Aunt Mei Ling. I won't be back till late, and Puri still won't be back for another week.'

'No problem for me,' I said, feeling really relieved that everything was happening just as I'd planned.

'Good. It's late now, Chee Seng. Maybe you'd better go to bed. I need to work on some papers for tomorrow. I've got a really important meeting with the board of directors. Sleep tight. I'll look in to see that you're asleep a bit later.'

As I lay down, the two Chee Sengs in my body did not feel very comfortable with each other. I had a job to silence their conflicting voices before I could sleep.

* * *

At school that Friday, Ka Ting was full of excitement about the party he'd planned for Saturday.

'It'll be the best ever! I've even got a band coming over. And this time some of the big guys will be there – they're the ones with the really hot stuff – plenty of fun for us all.' He laughed in a way that made me feel a bit uncomfortable. I realised that, half the time, I didn't really know what he meant when he talked about 'hot stuff' and 'fun', but I was fairly sure that some of it was illegal. But, for me, the party was not the main attraction. The most important thing was my plan to run away with Jessica. Everything else was just a means to that end.

I met Jessica in the library again before going home from school. 'Is everything OK for tomorrow?' I asked.

'No problem. I gave my backpack to Ka Ting and he'll keep it for me. Jane will drive me over for my going-away party around nine …'

'And I'll leave Swee Eng's a bit later, pick up my stuff from home, and take a taxi to Ka Ting's. I should be there by about ten thirty. Don't forget your passport. I can't wait to see you tomorrow.'

'Me neither,' she replied, and squeezed my hand as she left.

As I think back on the days that followed, the events seem to crowd in rapidly, one after the other. My memories are like a fast-moving film with one image flashing onto the screen for an instant, then being pushed aside by the next image.

Auntie Swee Eng picked me up at seven on Saturday evening. We spent another enjoyable evening together. She'd made me a special chicken curry with lots of tasty side dishes, and she played me some more classical music – this time Haydn and Bach. I began to understand how important music was for her. It was really part of her whole life, not something you just put on as a background. I wished I could learn to listen to it the way she did – with her whole self. One thing she said stuck in my mind. 'Music is such a comfort when you live on your own. You never feel lonely if you have great music.'

I was curious about the story she'd started to tell me the last time. 'I've been wondering about Mr Gana,' I said. 'How did you meet him?'

'It's funny how these things happen. I'm sure Daddy would have been horrified if he'd thought he'd been the one to blame. But in a sense he was.'

'How come?'

'Well, before he retired, he did one last tour of the country, looking at various agricultural projects, like rubber, oil palm and sugar cane plantations.[21] I was on holiday so he took me with him to Perak, up north. We spent a day visiting the rubber plantation where Gana was the assistant manager. That's when I took the first picture you saw. The British manager was away in the UK, so it was Gana who showed us round, and gave us lunch. As we were leaving, we looked at each other, and we knew. We knew that we loved each other. It sounds stupid and childish, doesn't it? I was only eighteen, not much older than you are now, but I knew I loved Gana, and all I could think of was how to spend the rest of my life with him. Later on, when we became lovers, he told me it had been the same for him. I wonder if you can understand that. Of course you can. Oh dear, where was I …?'

'So what happened then?'

'I wrote to him. He wrote to me. No emails or text messaging then! We had to be very careful, of course. Things were very different in those days. For one thing, most people didn't approve of marrying people from other communities. Gana was Indian, I was a Peranakan *nyonya*. Daddy would never have agreed. For another, people strongly disapproved of girls who had affairs with married men. Oh yes, Gana was married. His parents had arranged his marriage with a girl from back in India, Kerala I think. It had been a disaster. They didn't live together any more, but legally they were still married. I didn't think it mattered that much, but I knew it would cause a lot of trouble at home.'

'So what happened?' I asked. This story was starting to sound like a TV soap opera, a surprise every minute.

'Well, there was a big celebration at the golf club that year and a dance in the evening. I got a ticket for Gana. We spent the evening dancing together, talking … and I ran away with him the same evening! Can you believe that? How stupid I was, but how happy too. I stayed with him on the plantation for a month. It was the happiest time of my life – perhaps the only time I've ever been truly happy. We planned to set up home permanently together, so I went down to Kuala Lumpur to buy some things we needed. Gana was going to come down later. Daddy wouldn't let me come back home, so I stayed with my sister Rosie. She'd just got married. We were very close … we still are.'

'So did Gana come down to join you?' I asked.

She suddenly looked sad. 'I think we'd better leave all that for another time,' she replied. I thought I saw tears in her eyes and I didn't insist. We sat silently for a few minutes. Then she saw me checking my watch.

'Oh dear. Ten o'clock already. Time to take you home, young man.'

When we were in the car on the way home, she suddenly asked me, 'Are you all right?'

'Oh, yes,' I answered, but something in my voice must have sounded false.

'Are you sure? You seem a bit nervous this evening. If there's anything wrong, you can talk to me. I hope you know that. I don't want to stick my old nose into your life but …'

'No. It's OK. I was just thinking about Mum,' I mumbled, hating myself for this lie.

'Well, if everything's really all right, fine,' she said. 'But don't forget, I'm always there if you need to talk about anything – anything at all. Now, here we are. Sleep well and come and see me again next week.'

Chapter 13   *Pool party*

As soon as I got home that evening, I quickly packed the clothes and other things I'd prepared into my backpack. I took my laptop, just in case. I looked at all the small things I'd collected when I was a child – my shells, my coins, my Man. U. football posters. I would be leaving all this behind me. I picked up a kaleidoscope. It had been my favourite toy when I was about eight years old. I shook it and looked into it, watching the brightly coloured patterns. I shook it again and watched the patterns change. I couldn't help thinking that now my whole life was a kaleidoscope, a series of rapidly changing patterns as each event shook it.

I went to Mum's room. I knew she kept her cash in a drawer in her bedside table. The key was in a pot on her desk. I quickly unlocked the drawer. There was two thousand in fifty-ringgit notes in an envelope. I took a thousand, hoping she wouldn't notice anything missing immediately. It would be enough for Jessica and me to live on until we got to Thailand. My hands were trembling and my heart was beating like a drum. I was a thief, and I felt like one. It wasn't a good feeling but it was too late to feel sorry now.

I called Comfort Cabs and was soon on the highway going to Ka Ting's. It was just 11 pm.

When we stopped outside his house, there were a lot of very expensive-looking cars in the drive and the party was in full swing. I quickly found Ka Ting and he took me up to the room Jessica and I would share later. Her backpack was already there on a chair. I dropped my things in a corner and went over to Ka Ting, who was standing by the window. The room overlooked the terrace and the swimming pool.

A group of people were standing near the bar. Others were helping themselves to food. A few were dancing already. My heart missed a beat when I saw Jessica dancing with a man I'd never seen before. They were dancing very close, as if they knew each other well. I suddenly felt the sharp pain of jealousy for the first time.

Ka Ting took my hand and emptied three pills into it – one white, one blue and one pink. 'That should get you started,' he laughed. 'Everyone's getting really high already. Come and join the fun.' I thought for a moment. I hadn't taken any pills at the last party and I'd been fine. But when I'd taken them the first time I'd felt so bad afterwards. I smiled at Ka Ting and pushed the pills back into his hand.

'I don't need these to have fun,' I said, 'and neither should you.'

'OK, as you like.' He looked disappointed. 'But you don't know what you're missing.' We went downstairs and out onto the terrace. More people were dancing now. Some of them seemed to be out of control already, making wild movements and with strangely absent looks on their faces.

I saw Jessica again. She was still dancing with the same man. I looked at him more carefully. He looked about thirty years old, much older than me. He was dressed all in white. Even his shoes were white. His shirt collar was turned up and his shirt was unbuttoned to show a chest as hairy as a doormat. He wore lots of gold, including a thick gold chain round his neck and big rings on his fingers. He had a black moustache and carefully styled hair. I thought he looked like a gangster in a Bollywood film, and I took an immediate dislike to him. I waved at Jessica and she quickly stopped dancing and came over to me. 'What's going on?' I asked.

'What do you mean,' she replied, but she had a strange look in her eyes.

'Who's that? That guy you were dancing with. You look as if you know him pretty well.'

'Oh, don't be silly,' she laughed. 'That's just Suresh, someone I met at Ka Ting's last year. He owns an import-export business down in Klang. Come on. Let's dance. I feel dreamy already.' And she pulled me onto the dance floor. As we danced, I noticed the man watching us closely. I didn't like the way he was looking at us at all. Then he went away into a corner to talk to some other older guys. Some of the younger group went over to them, and I saw him handing over small packets of something. I also saw the flash of money changing hands.

When we sat down together in a dark corner, I tried to kiss Jessica but, for the first time, she turned her face away from me. 'Not now,' she complained. 'We'll have plenty of time later.' I was hurt but I tried not to show it.

As the party went on, I felt more and more uneasy. Too many people seemed to be acting strangely. Some of the older people were getting drunk. Others were obviously taking pills and getting the rush of excitement I remembered so well. I was glad I hadn't accepted the pills from Ka Ting. I decided to drink only water. I would need to keep a clear head, especially as Jessica had already passed the stage where she could think clearly. She'd obviously had something to drink, and from the dreamy look on her face, I could tell she'd taken some of Ka Ting's pills too.

I tried to keep her away from the crowd but she seemed to be drawn to them. I went to get her some food but when I came back she was dancing with that guy again. I didn't know what to do. After a time, I waved to her to come back, and after a few more minutes she came over to me, walking unsteadily. 'Wha's wrong?' she mumbled, speaking as if she had a piece of cotton wool in her mouth.

'Why are you dancing with him again?' I asked.

'I'm jus' havin' a bit of fun. Wha's wrong wi' that? You're no fun tonight. You goin' to a funeral or wha'?' and she smiled a silly smile.

'We should go upstairs,' I replied. 'We need to rest properly before we leave.'

'Tha's plenty o' time,' she said and started to walk away from me. She looked as if she might fall over at any moment. I took her hand and tried to pull her aside but she pushed me away. Once again she went over to the man I disliked the look of so much. Soon they were dancing again and he was holding her too close. I began to suspect that this was the man she'd told me about earlier – the one who had used her as a plaything. I could see he was wearing a wedding ring.

The music suddenly moved to a really hot rhythm and everyone joined in the dancing, except me. Ka Ting was leading the dance and he suddenly shouted, 'OK, everyone, in the pool.' And people began pulling off their clothes and jumping into the pool. I was shocked to see Jessica topless among them. In the pool there was a lot of splashing and fooling around. Things were getting out of control. I saw the man lift Jessica by the waist and drop her into the water. I watched, feeling helpless. But then, to my horror, I couldn't see Jessica any more! She had disappeared beneath the struggling crowd of bodies. Without thinking, I pulled off my shoes and trousers and dived in. The water was as warm as soup. I found Jessica lying in a corner at the bottom of the pool. People's legs were moving about above her. I managed to reach her and pull her to the surface. She was so heavy! Some people helped me drag her out of the pool and onto the terrace. She wasn't breathing!

Chapter 14 *Beyond parental control*

People started panicking immediately, running about aimlessly and screaming. I grabbed Ka Ting and shook him hard.

'Call the emergency services right away,' I ordered. 'Hurry!' I turned Jessica's body over and started to do mouth-to-mouth resuscitation. I was amazed that I could still remember how to do it from the first-aid course I'd done the year before. Then I put my hands on her chest and pushed hard – once, twice, three times.

After what seemed like ages, I felt a small movement in her lungs. Suddenly water came out of her mouth and she started breathing again. But she still didn't open her eyes. She was alive but something was badly wrong. I had a strange feeling now when I touched her – so very different from what I'd felt when we'd been lovers. Now it was all so impersonal. She felt like a total stranger, an object, no longer the girl of my dreams. And her skin felt cold, so cold.

A lot of the party-goers had hastily put on their clothes and were running to their cars. But an ambulance with flashing lights soon blocked the drive. It was closely followed by police motorbikes and a car full of uniformed men. 'Nobody leaves!' shouted a police officer. 'I want everyone inside the house. Now!'

The ambulance men took over from me and soon lifted Jessica into the back of the vehicle. As they closed the doors, I asked, 'Can I come with her? We're together …'

But I was pulled back into the house by two policemen. There was no point in trying to resist. I watched, helpless, as the ambulance drove away.

Inside the house, the policemen divided us into a teenage group and an older group. Each group was taken into a separate room. As my group was pushed roughly into the games room, Ka Ting whispered to me, 'Don't tell them anything about the pills, OK?' He looked terrified, no longer the confident, cheeky leader of all the fun and games. Now he was just a frightened boy.

A senior policeman, an inspector I think, came in after us. He shut the door behind him. 'This is serious,' he said. 'Very serious. A girl very nearly died here tonight. She may still die. We don't know what happened but we have our suspicions. If you know what's good for you, you'd better answer our questions honestly. If you try to cover things up, I can assure you that we will find out – and that won't be good for you. Understand?'

He stood there in his dark blue uniform with the silver buttons on his shoulders, slapping his stick impatiently against his leg. I felt sure he would have liked to have used the stick on us too. We all nodded. 'Right, now whose house is this?' After a brief pause, Ka Ting raised his hand nervously.

'How old are you?'

'I'm seventeen,' Ka Ting answered in a whisper.

'Seventeen, eh? And where are your parents? Do they know about this party here?'

'My dad's away in Hong Kong,' said Ka Ting. 'My mum doesn't live here any more.'

'And what's been going on here anyway? I want everyone to turn out their pockets. Now!' His voice was so loud we almost jumped out of our skins.

He walked up and down in front of us as we emptied the contents of our pockets onto the table, one at a time. The police put each lot into separate plastic bags. I felt relieved that I had not taken the pills from Ka Ting. When he emptied his pockets, there was a bag of pills and a lot of money.

'Right. I want everyone's name, address and contact telephone number. Now!' he shouted again. 'Give them to Sergeant Idris here. When we've got that information, and noted down what you had in your pockets, you'll be taken to the police station and held till tomorrow. Then we'll question you formally.'

By the time we left the room, several big police vans had arrived. Ten of us were pushed roughly into one of them and the rest of us into another. The doors banged shut and we were driven away. As we left, I saw the older people being pushed into two other vans. Some newspaper photographers were taking flash pictures. Someone must have phoned the press. The story would be in the Sunday newspapers. I hoped our names wouldn't be published.

We couldn't see much through the small windows, so I had no idea where they were taking us. About half an hour later, we stopped and the doors opened. A group of policemen pushed us through the door of a police station. Then we were locked into small cells, four people to a cell. I looked at my watch. It was three in the morning. I felt terrible. The others – the ones who had taken pills or drunk too much – felt even worse than me. I thought of Jessica, wondering where she was, and how she was... and who she really was. How could she have been in love with me when she had acted like that with Suresh? I thought of Mum and what she would do when she found out about all this. And I thought of Auntie Swee Eng and wished I was still safely at her house listening to music. It all seemed so long ago and so far away.

I felt dirty and tired. I badly wanted to relieve myself. When I called out to the policeman in the corridor to ask to use the toilet, he laughed.

'Where you think you are? Dis no Hilton Hotel, you know. You got one bucket, is for dat.' He pointed to a bucket in the corner of the cell. The four of us would have to share it. I relieved myself, feeling ashamed in front of the others. It was hot in the cells, and airless. We lay down on the hard wooden beds and tried to sleep. But sleep did not come. Instead, whenever I tried to close my eyes, all the events of the evening kept flashing in front of them.

At 7 am a guard came with a tray with some weak, half-cold tea, and a bowl of rice soup for each of us. That was all we got for breakfast. We were so hungry and thirsty that we ate it. Then we waited.

At about ten, they started to call out our names, one by one. It was eleven in the morning when my turn came. I was taken to a small bare room at the end of the corridor. The inspector was sitting behind a wooden table. There was just one weak electric light bulb hanging by a thin wire from the ceiling. A little light came in through a small barred window high up in the wall. I noticed a spider's web hanging from the high ceiling. There was a chair in front of the table. The inspector pointed to it, and I sat down.

'I don't want you to waste my time,' he began. 'I told you back at the house that I want straight answers to straight questions. The quicker you give me answers, the sooner you can be moved.'

I didn't like the sound of 'moved'. He hadn't said 'go home'. Moved? Moved to where? I'd heard about what happened to kids who were judged as 'beyond parental control'. They didn't go home; they went somewhere really bad.

'Name?'

'Yeo Chee Seng.'

He checked the paper in front of him. 'We'll be contacting your parents later. Is this your home number?' He read it out and I nodded. 'Who invited you to this party?'

'Ka Ting,' I replied.

'How do you know him?'

'We're in the same class at school,' I answered.

'How many people did you know at the party?' he asked, looking me directly in the eye. I looked down. 'Come on. How many?' he asked impatiently.

'Maybe four or five,' I mumbled

'What are their names?'

'Ka Ting, Chee Lick, Wendy, Ruby and Jessica, the girl who ...'

'Ah yes, Jessica,' he said thoughtfully. 'Tell me about Jessica.'

'She was my ... I mean, we were close friends. We were ...'

'She was your girlfriend, right?'

'Yes, sir.'

'And Ka Ting?'

'He invited us to the party – Jessica and me.'

'Had he ever invited you before, or was this the first time?'

'He'd invited me maybe twice before,' I confessed.

'What about these?' he asked, throwing some pills on the table. 'Do you know what they are?' It was useless to lie. He already knew the answer.

'Yes, sir. But those are not mine, sir.'

'I know that. Did Ka Ting ever give you this kind of thing before?'

'Erm …' I hesitated but it was useless.

'Right. He did. Where did he get them from, do you know?'

'No sir.'

'How about this guy? You know him at all?' He showed me a picture of the man Jessica had been dancing with. The man called Suresh.

'No sir. I saw him for the first time tonight. I just know his name is Suresh.'

'Did he give you anything? Sell you something maybe?'

'No sir,' I answered, truthfully.

'OK, I believe you,' he said. I felt relieved. 'Now you will go for a drugs test. If you test positive, some bad things are going to happen to you, my boy. Even if you test negative, we know you've taken them before.'

'Yes sir,' I admitted, looking down.

'Were you the one who gave the girl mouth-to-mouth?'

'Yes sir,' I said.

'Well, maybe that'll be good for you. You probably saved her life. But she's still in intensive care. She may not make it. And if not, someone will be in deep trouble,' he said, looking at the picture of Suresh. 'OK. Now you'll go back to your cell. I may call you again later.' He pointed to the door and a policeman led me back to my cell.

What happened between then and the time I was released the next afternoon? All I know is that Auntie Swee Eng came to the police station in Petaling Jaya to collect me on Monday afternoon. How did she manage that? She told me later that she'd known Inspector Sunderam (that was his name – the man who'd interviewed me) when she was younger. He owed her a favour. I never found out what the favour was, but she certainly knew how to take advantage of it! It was Swee Eng who somehow managed to persuade the police not to keep me in the cell, but to release me with a warning. She was now responsible for my behaviour. I was listed as being 'beyond parental control'. If I misbehaved again, she would have to answer to the police.

As we drove away from the police station, she squeezed my hand. 'Don't worry, Chee Seng,' she said in a kindly voice. 'I'll make sure you're OK. And your mum too … But … there's a lot to explain yet. I'd better tell you what's happened before we go to see her.' And she started to do just that.

Chapter 15   *Auntie Swee Eng takes charge*

In the taxi on the way to the hospital, Auntie Swee Eng told me what had happened. It seemed Mum had come back late on Saturday night. She'd been so tired that she'd gone to bed without checking if I'd been asleep or not. It was only on Sunday morning that she'd discovered I was gone. She'd called Auntie Swee Eng to check if I'd stayed with her on Saturday night. Auntie Swee Eng had come over straight away. Together they'd discovered that my things were missing. It was obvious that I'd run away. It was even more obvious when Mum discovered that some of her money was missing too!

'Your mother was so upset, Chee Seng. I'm not blaming you, but you really should know how badly it affected her. She was crying all the time. She couldn't stop. We even called your father in case you'd gone to him. Then he came over, which didn't improve things! They just started blaming each other for everything. Then we got a call from Jane, that nice sister of Jessica. She told us about Jessica's accident and the police raid and everything. You can imagine the effect that had on your mum. And then we read the report in *The Star* about Jessica's accident and the arrest of a lot of young drug users and some of the drug pushers. The headlines screamed about it – TEENAGE DRUG PARTY TRAGEDY. *The Straits Times* ran the story too – TRAGEDY AT

TEENAGE POOL PARTY. They didn't mention your name but we both knew you were up to your neck in trouble.'

I began to realise just how stupid and selfish I'd been. Auntie Swee Eng went on with her story. 'I started ringing around to see what I could find out. When I was younger, I had a good friend in the police. I soon found out where they were holding you. But I couldn't get to you before Monday. It was then that I found out it was Inspector Sunderam, my old friend, who was on the case. That's when I came over and got you out. Sunderam always had a soft heart. I only had to remind him of something he'd been involved in when he was young for him to let you go with a warning.'

I realised just how lucky I'd been. If it hadn't been for Auntie Swee Eng, I might still have been locked up in that police cell, with no hope of a quick release.

'But I'm sorry, Chee Seng, there's something awful I have to tell you. Your mum is in the central hospital, in the intensive care unit. She took a whole bottle of sleeping pills last night. Luckily, she called me when she had second thoughts about what she'd done and I managed to get her to hospital. She's unconscious now and we don't know whether she'll recover.'

I suddenly felt the earth collapse under me. I'd run away, and Mum had tried to take her own life! I couldn't think straight. What had I done? How could I ever forgive myself?

Auntie Swee Eng took my hand. 'I'm sorry, Chee Seng. I know it's hard for you. But please don't think it's only your fault. Things like this happen when someone gets hit by one thing after another. Your mother has been suffering from what your father did when he left you. She's had the worry of trying to bring you up all by herself. And all sorts of problems at work. I didn't know, and neither did you, but last Friday they dismissed her. It was all about office politics but her job was gone. That meant she didn't know how she would manage for money in future. She was desperate. Then, yesterday, she found out you'd run away and got into trouble with the police, and she cracked. Sometimes, people crack up when the pressure gets too much for them. You're not to blame, your mum's not to blame – it's life that's to blame – if "blame" is the right word for it. It's the way things sometimes are. Things happen.'

The taxi was entering the gates of the central hospital as she spoke, and I knew that something terrifying was going to happen to me again. I hated hospitals. I hated their smell and the atmosphere of fear.

Chapter 16   *Picking up the pieces*

So here we are, waiting. A doctor comes into the waiting room. He looks kind but he has a concerned expression on his face.

'Good morning, I'm Doctor Ong,' he says as he sits down with us. 'I'm afraid your mother is still in a serious condition. We're doing our best for her, but she took a very big overdose of pills. She's stable at the moment but we won't really be able to tell you anything more till tomorrow. I think the best thing you can do is to go home and wait till we call you. I'm sorry I can't tell you any more than that for now.'

As we arrive back home, everything seems so familiar and so strange at the same time. I left here only two nights ago, thinking it was the last time I'd see it, and here I am back again.

And there, standing at the front door, to welcome us with her usual cheerful smile, is Puri. Puri is back! Apparently she came back last night, in the middle of all this trouble. 'Hello, Chee Seng,' she says. 'I make you some special fish and chips, and banana fritters for dessert …' Just like old times. And, of course, she says nothing about Mum. No one wants to mention what's happened – yet.

Auntie Swee Eng has decided to move over here till we know what's happening with Mum. She moves into the spare room, right next to mine. I feel somehow protected to know she is there so close to me. She unpacks her bag and comes downstairs to sit with me before dinner. She's brought a few CDs with her, and puts one on. It's a piece by Handel. I thought that Handel had written the *Messiah* and that was all, so I'm amazed at this piece called the *Water Music*. Auntie Swee Eng tells me the story of how King George I of England asked Handel to write it, and how it was played on boats on the Thames.

The telephone rings. We both rush to answer it, but it isn't someone about Mum; it's Jane. Jessica is out of danger and recovering in a private hospital. Would I like to see her? I say I'll call tomorrow. Mum is my first priority.

* * *

Later, after dinner, I ask Auntie Swee Eng, 'I've been wondering – how did the story of Mr Gana end?'

'All right. I'll tell you. Everyone likes to know what happened in the end, don't they? Well, the British manager came back. Gana was due for leave. He was driving to Ipoh to catch the train to join me in Kuala Lumpur. It was evening and the road was dark. It was raining heavily. Somehow the car hit a tree and he was killed on the spot.'

I don't know what to say. It seems so cruel. But there's more to come.

'My sister Rosie told me about it. She'd seen it in the newspaper. I couldn't bear to read about it or look at the photographs of the crash. I didn't sleep for days, and I think I cried till there were no more tears left in my body. My life was over.'

'But you said you went to Singapore,' I say. 'How was that?'

'I'm not sure I should be telling you this. I suppose I might as well now that I've gone this far. It's many years since I've talked about it. Everyone in the family just wanted to forget about it all. But you see, soon after Gana was killed, I found out that I was expecting his child. Daddy had to be told. He was furious of course. He called a family meeting. They all agreed I should be sent to Singapore to get me out of the way and stop any gossip. So that's what happened.'

There are tears in her eyes. I cannot ask her what happened in Singapore, and she doesn't offer to tell me. Enough is enough, I guess. Some things are better left unsaid.

'It's getting late, Chee Seng,' she says. 'I'm sorry if I've upset you with my story. It wasn't the end of my life, you know. Who knows whether Gana and I would have been happy together anyway? Maybe not. And as for Daddy and the family, well, I forgave them long ago. But, as you can see, I cannot forget. I never married. Instead I became everyone's aunt. All right. You'd better get to bed now. Sleep well, Chee Seng.'

She leans over and kisses me lightly on the cheek. As I go upstairs, she starts to play the *Water Music* again …

It's late but I'm still lying awake in my bed. I can't get Auntie Swee Eng's story out of my head. I wonder how someone can live through what she's experienced in her life without going completely crazy. But then I start to think of the rest of us too. Will Mum be all right? How will she cope when she comes out of hospital – if she gets better? How will Jessica cope with her life too? How will Dad cope with the crisis he's caused? And how will I cope with the consequences of what I did? All the faces and actions and scenes go round in my head like the coloured shapes in my old kaleidoscope. They make one pattern, then, as I go on thinking, they break up and make different, changing patterns. At last I fall asleep, but the changing images go on troubling my dreams.

* * *

Next morning, there's a call from the hospital. Mum has regained consciousness! She's out of danger. We can visit her that afternoon. What a relief!

When we arrive, she's sitting up in bed drinking something from a glass. The curtains are open and the room is full of light. They've taken away all the tubes from her nose and arms. She's smiling weakly. She has black bags under her eyes, and her arms are bruised blue and yellow, but she looks more like her old self again.

'Hello, Mum,' I say, a bit embarrassed. 'You're looking better.' Suddenly a wave of love sweeps over me and I rush into her open arms. 'I'm sorry, Mum,' I cry. 'I'm so, so sorry.'

She is crying too, but crying with relief. She looks at Auntie Swee Eng and says, 'Swee Eng, thank you so much for everything. What would we have done without you?' Auntie Swee Eng smiles and quietly leaves us alone.

Mum and me have a long talk. I try to tell her as much as I can about all the stuff that's happened. I even tell her about Jessica – though not all of it! Thank goodness, she doesn't ask. But most important, she'll be coming home soon. Home.

Then she talks to me about Dad. 'Did you know your father has been to see me? He told me he's split up with Auntie Veena, you know. She's gone back to Uncle Krish.'

'No, I didn't know,' I say.

'He wants to come back home,' she says. 'What do you think?'

I hesitate before answering. To tell the truth, I'm not at all comfortable with the idea of having him back. But I'm not sure how she feels, so I say, 'I don't know, Mum. I think about him a lot but … It seems a bit strange now. I mean, after everything that's happened and … I mean, how would we get back to normal again?'

'Don't worry,' she says. 'I've told him I don't want him back. Certainly not right away. It's too soon. And maybe I won't want him back at all … after everything he's done to us. I still can't forgive him for that.'

'No …' is all I can say.

'But he's still your father,' she says. 'Maybe you should think about seeing him sometimes. I know he misses you a lot. It's up to you though. Just think about it, that's all.'

*　*　*

Now we live each day as it comes. Auntie Swee Eng has spoken to the school principal and they've decided it will be better for me not to go back to school, at least not till Mum comes home. I may have to repeat a year though. But every day Swee Eng gives me schoolwork to do – really interesting stuff – books to read that I've never heard of before, problems to solve. I hadn't realised she'd been a teacher herself for thirty years! It's a lot better than school actually. And every day we go to visit Mum. The doctor says she could be home by next week.

As we're coming out of the hospital, I see Dad arriving, with a big bunch of roses. I feel confused about him. I'm still not sure I want him back.

In the evening, Dad calls me. He wants us to meet somewhere. I don't really want to meet him but he's very insistent. So we agree to meet the next afternoon at the *kopitiam*[22] a few blocks from home. I certainly don't want him coming over to the house! The *kopitiam* is quiet at that time between the lunchtime rush and the evening crowd of hungry families. We sit at a small table outside. He orders sweet *teh tarik*[23] for himself and a large *ice kacang*[24] for me; the broken ice stained with red and green juices. 'I want you to listen carefully,' he says, as we get down to the serious part of the conversation. 'I know I've hurt you – and your mum. There's not much I can do about that except to say I'm sorry. And I really am sorry. There's no point in looking for excuses for what I did because there aren't any. Maybe one day, like me, you'll find you've started something that you can't stop. You know it's not right, but you're too far in to stop.'

I think about me and Jessica. I think I understand what he means. I've been almost as crazy as him in my own way. And I've hurt Mum too, so I'm certainly not innocent. But I still feel angry with him for what he did. Maybe if he hadn't run off with Auntie Veena, none of the rest would have happened. But maybe it would have anyway ... I feel confused. As Swee Eng says, 'Things happen.'

Dad is still talking. 'I've asked Mum to have me back, to let me move in with you again. She says it's too soon. What do you say?' What can I say? I dig into my *ice kacang*, which is rapidly melting in the afternoon heat.

'I don't know, Dad,' I mumble, without looking up.

'Well, look. I've told Mum she won't have to worry about money any more. So she won't need to work and that will take some of the pressure off her. And we're thinking about putting you into the international school, when the new year starts. You can have private teaching till then. I've told Mum I'll pay for it. Meanwhile, I think you and I should meet regularly, maybe every weekend. We can do something together like we used to, if you like. What do you think?'

Does he think he can buy us back? I'm not sure I like this idea. And I hate him for talking with Mum about me behind my back. 'Maybe, Dad, but not yet. Mum has to get better. And I don't know about meeting.

I'm sorry but you don't feel like the same person to me any more…'

He doesn't insist but he's clearly disappointed. What does he expect me to do – jump up and kiss him or something? He still doesn't know that I saw him in the bedroom with Auntie Veena. Maybe it's better if he doesn't find out. Before I leave he says, 'What do you want for your birthday this year, Chee Seng? It's coming up next Sunday.'

I've forgotten all about my birthday, what with all the things that have happened. Again it sounds as if he's trying to buy me back. I hate that. Anyway, I can't think of anything I want. 'Don't worry about it, Dad,' I say.

As I walk away, he calls out, 'I'll call you, right?' I nod but keep on walking without looking back.

* * *

The days slip by so fast now. It's already Friday, nearly a week since Jessica and I planned to run away. I call Jane. I like Jane and I've been thinking a lot about Jessica. It seems she's out of danger now and will soon be going home. Then what, I wonder.

Jane picks me up the same afternoon. On the way to the private hospital, we talk. 'So, Chee Seng, how are you now? How can I ever thank you for saving Jessica's life? If you hadn't dived in, she'd have drowned.'

'It was just lucky,' I say. But I'm really thinking that it's lucky Jane doesn't know everything!

'Lucky? Maybe. Did you know she almost died from the mixture of pills she took? But I wonder where she got the drugs from. Not from you, I hope?'

'No, not from me.'

'The police are still holding some of the suspects though, including Ka Ting, and that Suresh character … a nasty piece of work. In fact, both of them are.'

I change the subject. 'How is Jessica now?'

'She's over the worst,' says Jane. 'They say she'll be able to go home early next week. Mum and Dad will take her to Australia in a couple of weeks' time when she's well enough to travel.' I don't reply. I just let the information sink in. Strangely, I feel almost relieved to know that Jessica will soon be gone.

Jessica is in a room of her own at the hospital. She has a lot of pillows behind her. Her face is so white, and her eyes have dark rings around them. She smiles as I come in. Jane tactfully finds an excuse to leave us alone for a while. I wonder how much she actually knows about Jessica and me. 'How are you, Jessica?' I ask. It's a stupid question but what else can I say?

'I'm all right now, Chee Seng', she replies, with a tired smile. 'I ache all over and I was being sick a lot at first, but now I'm basically OK.'

'I'm glad,' I say. But I realise that I don't really care so much about Jessica any more. I wonder how she feels about me.

'Chee Seng, they say that you saved my life. I still don't remember properly what happened at the pool … but thank you. I really mean that.'

'Well, somehow you must have been pushed under the water with all those people. You'd had quite a lot to drink, I think, and too many different pills. Anyway, you were behaving strangely all evening.'

'I'm sorry, Chee Seng. I think it was all the pressure about running away. Funny to think that we really thought we could run away to Thailand, isn't it? It was just a childish dream really.'

'I suppose so,' I agree, 'but it didn't feel like it at the time.'

'Not for me either. Now they're going to send me to Australia anyway. Maybe it's best after all. What do you think?'

'Maybe,' I say, but there is still a question burning my tongue. I have to ask her. 'What about Suresh? Is he the man you had the trouble with last year?'

She reaches out and takes my hand. 'Yes, he is. I don't know what got into me that night. It was so stupid after the way he treated me before. I don't know why I did it. Why would I act like that? I still don't understand it myself. I still… I like you, you know.'

'I like you too,' I reply, but we both know that things will never be the same between us. And I think we are both relieved.

As I get out of the car outside my house, Jane touches my arm. 'Chee Seng, I know what happened. I don't blame you. But I think it's best for everyone if Jessica goes away. It's time to grow up now. But don't be angry with her, or with us. And do stay in touch. We like you. And Jessica will miss you. Don't forget us …' And she drives off.

* * *

The next day is Saturday. I notice a lot of whispering between Auntie Swee Eng and Puri, and they go out to the market and come back loaded with bags. Then there's a lot of activity in the kitchen. Something's going on.

When I get up on Sunday morning, Auntie Swee Eng has already left. Puri says she doesn't know where she's gone, but I'm sure she does really. Meanwhile, Puri is busy in the kitchen preparing I don't know what. Around midday,

Auntie Swee Eng comes back. She opens the passenger door of her car and out steps … Mum! Mum is back! Puri runs out to welcome her. I carry her bag into the house and upstairs to her room.

Mum and Auntie Swee Eng and Puri stand in a line in front of the kitchen door. Delicious smells are coming from the kitchen. We're going to have a really special lunch, that much is sure! Then Mum hands me an envelope with a card in it. 'Happy birthday, Chee Seng,' she says, and gives me a warm hug. Then she points at a package on the hall table. 'Open it. It's your present. I think you may have lost the other one …'

I obey, and untie the string and unpack … a state-of-the-art laptop. I feel my face glowing hot with embarrassment. I left my laptop at Ka Ting's that night. I never got it back. Maybe it's somewhere in the police station. Maybe it's still there along with my backpack. But how did Mum know it was missing? And I wonder how much Auntie Swee Eng knows. Maybe Sunderam told her about the one I left behind!

Now it's Auntie Swee Eng's turn. She hands me a package wrapped in red paper and tied with gold ribbon. 'Happy birthday, Chee Seng. Open it.' I carefully untie the ribbon and unwrap the paper. Inside there's a leather-covered photo album. I open it to the first page, and there's the photograph of my great-grandparents. I turn the page and find a picture of my grandparents. Then of my parents, my uncles, my aunts, myself as a baby … There is just one picture of Auntie Swee Eng with Gana. 'I thought you might like to keep it going,' says Auntie Swee Eng, with a smile. 'We're in this together, don't forget. There are plenty more pages to fill.'

I feel like crying but I just give her a big hug.

Then Puri holds out a small package wrapped in brown paper. 'I bring for you from my country' she says. 'I hope you like. My sister she make for you.' I open it carefully. Inside there is a beautifully decorated cotton shirt. 'You try maybe?' she suggests.

I go to the bedroom and slip it on. It fits me perfectly, and I feel like a prince in it. 'It's lovely,' I say, and I wear it for the rest of the day.

We have a wonderful lunch, cooked by Puri and Auntie Swee Eng, all my favourite dishes. *Sotong*[25] with ladies' fingers[26] and a lovely red pepper sauce, curried chicken, *asam laksa*, steamed sea bass[27] with lime and garlic, roast duck with thin pancakes – there is hardly room on the table for all the food. And the meal ends with a cake – and what a cake it is! It's made with a rich mixture of raisins,[28] nuts and spices like cinnamon and ginger. The covering is cream. It's a dream cake! We attack it till nothing is left.

A bit later in the afternoon, I'm surprised when Faisal, Ka Choon and Dev come by. I feel bad about the way I treated them. But they have presents for me too. Dev has brought me a brand-new basketball. Faisal has framed one of his paintings for me. Ka Choon gives me the latest computer game. I feel great. They are my real, true friends, even if I treated them badly. We go up to the park together and play basketball till it starts to get dark.

Just before dinner, when I get back, there's a ring at the door. Puri goes to answer it. It's Dad. He comes in carrying a small bamboo cage. He puts it down carefully and undoes the door. A small puppy jumps out. He's like a ball of soft wool, warm and playful. He looks a little bit like Raj, and my heart aches as I pick him up. I thank Dad. Mum's upstairs but doesn't come down until Dad leaves.

Now I'm seventeen. I know that my family loves me. I have a dog again – and this time I'll take better care of him. And last, but not least, I know that I'm part of a long history of happenings, some good, some painful. I know that things are not always what they seem. I know we all need to be forgiven for something. But I know that we can sometimes forgive, yet be unable to forget. I know that love is not always what it seems to be. I know 'things happen' but I also know they happen to people, and people are sometimes strong enough to rise above events. And I know, above all, that I do not know what will happen next … I'm seventeen now and there's plenty of time left for things to happen!

Later in the evening, Dad phones. 'Chee Seng,' he says. 'Happy birthday. I love you, you know, whatever you may think. Can we have lunch together next Saturday? I'd really like that.'

'Let me think about it,' I say. 'Maybe.'

Glossary

1 **samosa:** small Indian pastry with spicy meat or vegetable filling.
2 **satay:** small pieces of grilled meat (chicken or beef) on sticks, served with peanut sauce.
3 **beef rendang:** spicy cubes of beef in a thick, rich sauce.
4 **tofu:** a substance similar to cheese, used in many Chinese dishes, made from soya beans.
5 **asam laksa:** a fish stew, flavoured with tamarind and other spices, served with noodles.
6 **tamarind:** the fruit of a tree common in India and southeastern Asia, eaten fresh or used in cooking.
7 **Selangor:** the state within which Kuala Lumpur lies.
8 **sari:** a long dress worn by Indian women.
9 **noodles:** long thin strips made from flour or rice dough, cooked in boiling water.
10 **taro:** a root vegetable commonly used in Asian dishes.
11 **mango:** a sweet fruit with yellow flesh.
12 **nyonya:** woman from the Peranakan (Straits Chinese) community.
13 **kebaya:** a kind of blouse, often made of lace. Worn with the sarong by nyonyas.
14 **sarong:** a piece of cloth which is wrapped around the waist to form an ankle-length skirt.
15 **Punjabi:** something or someone from the Punjab region of India.

16 **lorong:** Malay word for a small road.

17 **Federal Highway:** the main highway running from the south to the north of Malaysia.

18 **mangosteen:** a sweet white fruit inside a thick, dark purple skin.

19 **ringgit:** unit of Malaysian currency.

20 **gula melaka:** a dessert made from the sago plant, with brown sugar, coconut milk and ice.

21 **plantation:** a large area where crops like rubber, sugar cane, tea and coffee are grown.

22 **kopitiam:** a neighbourhood coffee shop where people meet to eat, chat and exchange gossip.

23 **teh tarik:** sweet milky tea flavoured with cinnamon.

24 **ice kacang:** sweet and highly coloured juices poured over broken ice.

25 **sotong:** a seafood dish made from squid.

26 **ladies' finger (okra):** a sticky vegetable.

27 **sea bass:** a kind of saltwater fish.

28 **raisin:** a dried grape, used in many dishes.

Malaysia: some brief information

Malaysia has a rich mix of people, cultures and languages:

The **Orang Asli** are the original inhabitants of the region, now forming about 11% of the population. They speak a variety of languages.

The **Malays,** who speak Malay, are Muslim. They make up about 50% of the population.

The **Chinese** came from the south of China in the 19th century. They are the most business-oriented group in Malaysia. Some are Christians, others are Buddhists or Taoists. They number about 24% of the population.

The **Indians** worked in the rubber estates during British rule. They came mainly from southern India. There are other Indian groups such as the Punjabi Sikhs. Together, they make up 7 or 8% of the population.

The **Peranakans** (Straits Chinese) have a rich culture which evolved from the intermarriage of 15th century Chinese traders who came to Melaka, with Malay women. The men are called 'babas' and the women 'nyonyas'. Their language, Baba Malay, is distinctive, as is their costume and food. Today there is a revival in Peranakan culture.

Malaya became part of the British Empire in the 19th century. It was occupied by the Japanese during World War II, then fought for independence from Britain (granted in 1957). The new state of Malaysia was formed in 1963. Malaysia is a lively, multicultural society. It is a popular tourist destination with beautiful beaches and islands, interesting traditions and handicrafts, and wonderfully varied food.

Cambridge English Readers

If you liked *The Best of Times?*, you may also want to read other titles at Level 6:

Nelson's Dream
by J.M. Newsome
Nelson Mbizi returns to his home in southern Africa after studying in Britain. When he tries to help a family of orphans he meets Viki, a South African TV presenter. The story of Nelson and Viki's relationship is told against a background of HIV/AIDS and government corruption on the one hand, and great humour and wonderful music on the other.

He Knows Too Much
by Alan Maley
An English company executive in India is dismissed after he tries to uncover corruption within his company. He returns to England where his life falls apart and his marriage breaks up. He then sets out on a one-man search for the truth behind his dismissal. He turns to the rich mystery and beauty of India and is finally forced to choose between love and revenge.

Murder Maker
by Margaret Johnson
After being jilted by her lover, Carla is devastated and intends to seek revenge. She joins a self-help group for people in similar situations and there she meets three women who have been betrayed or abandoned by their husbands. Carla decides to rehearse her revenge on these men and starts by buying a ticket to Cuba.

All Cambridge English Readers are available as eBooks and audiobooks. For more information visit www.cambridge.org/elt/readers